The ART *of* SUCCESS

The ART *of* SUCCESS

21 MANTRAS FROM THE BHAGAVAD GITA

J.S. MISHRA

B L O O M S B U R Y

NEW DELHI • LONDON • OXFORD • NEW YORK • SYDNEY

BLOOMSBURY INDIA
Bloomsbury Publishing India Pvt. Ltd
Second Floor, LSC Building No. 4, DDA Complex,
Pocket C – 6 & 7, Vasant Kunj,
New Delhi 110070

BLOOMSBURY, BLOOMSBURY QUEST and the Diana logo are trademarks of Bloomsbury Publishing Plc

First published in India 2019
This edition published in 2025

ISBN: 978-93-69525-80-5
2 4 6 8 10 9 7 5 3 1

Printed and bound in India by Replika Press Pvt. Ltd.

To find out more about our authors and books, visit www.bloomsbury.com and sign up for our newsletters

In sacred remembrance of my parents,
Smt. Rajeshwari Mishra &
Shri Sabhajeet Mishra

Contents

Preface

All institutions—whether a family, group, community, organisation, or country—require the presence of a leader: someone who can make decisions and act righteously on behalf of the institution. Every individual—whether a child, parent, elder or teacher— plays the role of a leader at some stage in his life.

Emphasizing the importance of leadership, Krishna says in the Bhagavad Gita:

यद्यदाचरति श्रेष्ठस्तत्तदेवेतरो जनः।
स यत्प्रमाणं कुरूते लोकस्तदनुवर्तते।।

(अध्याय 3/21)

Yadyadaacharati shreṣhṭhastattadevetaro janaḥ
Sa yatpramaṇam kurute lokastadanuvartate

(Chapter- 3/21)

(Whatever a great man does, others imitate; whatever standard he sets, the world follows.)

A leader is a visionary who defines reality, and enables the team to translate its dreams into actuality. This requires creativity in thought, speech and action. The absence of such a personality often leads to suffering for communities, societies and countries. The role of a leader becomes especially critical in times of grave challenges and adversities. At such times, a leader of foresight and equanimity is required. History bears testimony to the fact that great leaders have guided their people through the most challenging times with the sheer strength of their character.

While we all want others to change, the irony is that nobody is willing to change themselves, even if it means elevating their own consciousness. Perhaps the greatest challenge for a leader, is to inspire people to assess their own strengths and weaknesses, to build upon their strengths, and overcome their limitations. For bringing about this change in the people, the leader ought to treat them with empathy, integrity and emotional intelligence. The Gita teaches that true leadership begins with deep self-understanding, confidence and awareness of his potential and the goals of the organization.

No one is born a leader; leadership skills can be and must be cultivated. Family, educational institutions, life experiences, exposure to diverse ideas and travel all contribute significantly to the making of a leader.

A very important aspect of leadership is teamwork. A true leader must set aside personal ego, share credit generously, and encourage the team to work as one unit. To unify a team, it is important for the leader to understand that each individual member of the team is shaped by their unique life circumstances—family background, geographical location, value system, education, traditions, and culture. In today's interconnected world, revolutionary changes in information technology have brought people across the world much closer, and in instant contact with one another despite geographical divides.

However, social, cultural, economic and educational differences affect attitudes and responses of people to the same situations. A leader must account for these diversities and devise suitable policies, strategies and practices accordingly.

The sages and seers of ancient India understood these eternal truths and gave shape to these values, beliefs and ideals in the scriptures like the Vedas, Upanishads, Ramayana, Mahabharata and Bhagavad Gita. These scriptures unfold the vast canvas of society and offer timeless guidance on thought, conduct and behaviour to people.

The story of Lord Rama as described in the Ramayana, by Maharshi Valmiki, is one such example that has influenced generations regarding human values, traditions, righteous conduct and relationships with family, friends and allies. The great epic Mahabharata, authored by Maharishi Vyas, has strongly impacted the psyche of people in India regarding ethics and morals, beliefs and conduct, and the disastrous consequences of unchecked desires like ego, jealousy, lust, greed and anger. The Bhagavad Gita has transcended generations, inspiring scholars and leaders across the world – R.W. Emerson, Henry David Thoreau, B. G. Tilak, Mahatma Gandhi, Albert Einstein and Nelson Mandela among them. Lessons derived from the Gita remain as relevant today as they were five thousand years ago.

The teachings of the Gita, are of universal significance as far as human values and ideals go, inspiring equally a commoner, a seeker as well as a leader to understand the realities of life, perform actions without bothering about results. The Gita offers a philosophy, right perspective, and a proper worldview to make life virtuous and meaningful. This scripture presents the philosophy of life as a poetic recitation and dialogue between two friends, Krishna and Arjuna, the two most prominent figures that dominate the great canvas of the Mahabharata. The verses of the Gita are a lighthouse of intellect and wisdom, and have great potential for guiding human beings through the turmoil of daily life in today's complex world.

The Gita has influenced thoughts, actions and lives of people through generations but it has not been much studied in the context of leadership and management principles. Its teachings are most relevant in the modern context for leaders working in public affairs, corporate world as well as in various organisations and institutions. The Gita stands as the ultimate self-help guide applicable in every sphere of life. It teaches how to act with vigour and sincerity while remain detached from the fruits of one's actions.

It is a generally accepted fact about the Gita that whenever it is studied with devotion and concentration, it gives the reader a new energy, a new joy and a new vision. It has a natural flow of questions and answers. Arjuna, despite being a prince of royal lineage and a great warrior of his time, never hesitates in asking questions and comes across as a person ever keen to know the mysteries of life and human nature. He seeks solutions to various doubts and queries, and Krishna, his friend and mentor offers a practical roadmap not only for worldly success and acclaim but also for realising higher consciousness.

The teachings of the Gita are relevant for almost every conceivable context of life, be it spiritual, professional or managerial. Its lessons remain relevant in all real-life situations. The Gita has revolutionised the consciousness of human beings by its emphasis on detached action and no expectation for the fruit of one's actions.

The Art of Success – 21 Mantras from the Bhagavad Gita is an expression of the belief that the teachings of the Gita are eternally relevant. Its wisdom not only enhances daily life but also builds leadership grounded in vision, strength and balance. It is my hope that this book will introduce the readers to new dimensions of thought, deepen leadership skills, and inspire a new worldview. It may open new vistas for understanding oneself and guide a reader in exploring an entirely new life and new destiny.

May this effort help readers enrich their personal lives, understand people better, and evolve a new style of leadership. It has the potential to mitigate the anxieties and complexities brought about by the ever-accelerating pace of life. May the teaching of the Gita guide you to peace, clarity, and success.

Jai Shankar Mishra

Lucknow

Acknowledgements

This book would not have been possible without the unwavering support and encouragement of my close family and friends. I offer my heartfelt thanks and deep gratitude to each one of them.

First and foremost, I express my sincere appreciation to my wife, Sharda for her enduring patience, warmth and care during many long hours spent at the computer. More importantly, I thank her for being a steadfast partner and source of strength for over four decades.

I appreciate my elder son, Abhishek, whose insightful advice helped shape the direction of the book. He urged me to distil lessons from the Gita that could serve as practical guidelines for maintaining calm and balance in daily life, and help achieve the elusive work-life equilibrium. My daughter Prashasti, and younger son, Divya the admirers of all my creative pursuits deserve special thanks for their love and prompt, thoughtful feedback on the manuscript.

The draft benefited greatly from the discerning eye and constructive suggestions of Alpha Jayanti Singh. I extend my special thanks to her for her invaluable assistance in finalising the text, structure and title of the book.

My thanks are also due to Paul Vinay Kumar and Jyoti Mehrotra for their kind support and encouragement throughout this journey. A word of appreciation is due to Rajiv Beri the Managing Director of Bloomsbury, for his cooperation and support in bringing this work to fruition.

This revised edition of *The Art of Success: 21 Mantras from the Bhagavad Gita* would not have been possible without the active guidance of Mr Paul Vinay Kumar, Publisher – Special Projects, Bloomsbury. I am also thankful to Rajbilochan Prasad and Satyabrat Mishra for their sincere efforts in shaping the book into an attractive and impressive publication.

Finally, I extend my heartfelt gratitude to the entire team at Bloomsbury for their exemplary dedication and care in producing this book with such finesse. Their collective effort has given it the quality and presentation it truly deserves.

Success Mantra 1

Everyone Loves to Work

Work is fundamental to human nature. It is the foundation of all success and the driver behind the evolution of civilization and culture. Yet it is a common perception persisting in many organizations that people are lazy and do not want to work. This attitude creates an unfriendly and hostile environment, and leads to a trust deficit between management and subordinates. This creates negative impression and eventually, the belief gets propagated and entrenched in the minds of senior managers in the organisation. They then start looking at them with suspicion and a preconceived notion that employees are, in fact, lazy, inefficient and disinclined to work. This, in turn, hinders peace and harmony in the organization. In such an environment, no great objective can be achieved, no matter how great the leader may be.

The Bhagavad Gita emphasizes the viewpoint that a human being cannot remain without working even for a moment. The very basic nature of a human being is to work, and given the right settings and motivation, everybody would work keenly.

This wisdom is enshrined in the Gita in the following shloka:

न हि कश्चित्क्षणमपि जातु तिष्ठत्यकर्मकृत् ।
कार्यते ह्यवशः कर्म सर्वः प्रकृतिजैर्गुणैः ।।

(अध्याय 3 / 5)

Na hi kaschitkshanamapi jaatu tishthatyakarmakrit
Kaaryate hyavashah karma sarvah prakrtijairgunaih.

(Chapter 3/5)

(Surely, none can remain inactive even for a moment; for everyone is helplessly driven to action by the impulses of nature.)

According to the Gita, everybody is a natural worker, as the very nature of a human being impels him to work. To remain idle even for a short time is difficult for humans. Inactivity is unnatural to human beings. It is neither true nor wise to think that people are lazy and do not want to work.

This thought is beautifully reflected by William Wordsworth as well:

The eye cannot choose but see,
We cannot bid the ear be still.
Our bodies feel where'er they be,
Against or with our will.

It is true that without work, it is not possible to live and sustain a meaningful life. There have been many scientific studies that have proven the association between lack of occupation and deterioration in mental and physical health. Thus, leaders must shed preconceived notions about employees' willingness to work and recognize the inherent drive in every human being.

Leaders and managers need to understand and respect the individuality of workers and promote an environment of trust; only then will brotherhood, empathy and camaraderie can prevail. It is obvious that a trust-deficit environment does not serve any purpose and should be discouraged. It is a great obstacle in the path of significant achievement and leads to avoidable conflict and disharmony in the organization.

Krishna, in the Gita, tells Arjuna that even in waking moments, the human mind is constantly occupied with thought of work. He further stresses this in the following shloka:

कर्मेन्द्रियाणि संयम्य य आस्ते मनसा स्मरन्।
इन्द्रियार्थान्विमूढात्मा मिथ्याचारः स उच्यते।।

(अध्याय 3/6)

Karmendriyaani sanyamya ya aaste manasaa smaran
Indriyaarthaan vimoodhaatmaa mithyaachaarah sa uchyate.

(Chapter 3/6)

(He who outwardly restrains the organs of action but continues to mentally dwell on sense objects is deluded and is called a hypocrite.)

The Gita does not advocate inaction of any type and the above shloka abhors such a man by addressing him as a hypocrite.

There has been a tradition where people undergoing suffering in life due to some tragedy or fascination for ascetic life renounce worldly duties and join the order of asceticism. Many of them later realize that it's not natural to withdraw from life and the world. Consequently, they remain engrossed with the ways of worldly life but outwardly pose as an ascetic. Such people apparently do not indulge in life's chores as a householder, but mentally they are very much with the world. That's why Krishna calls them hypocrites and men of false conduct.

The secret of civilization and evolution of mankind lies in working–with love, devotion and commitment. No dream can ever become a reality just by thinking about it; it takes sound planning, hard work and firm determination to realize it. The great monuments, poetry, music and masterpieces of painting are all examples of tremendous vision and acts performed with immense love and devotion.

Leadership, too, is not a matter of title or position but of inspiration, influence, and impact - achieved through one's own dedication to meaningful work.

Krishna extols the virtues of active engagement once again in the following shloka:

यस्त्विन्द्रियाणि मनसा नियम्यारभतेऽर्जुन।
कर्मेन्द्रियैः कर्मयोगमसक्तः स विशिष्यते।।

(अध्याय 3/7)

Yas tvindriyaani manasaa niyamyaarabhatearjuna
Karmendriyaih karmayogamasaktah sa vishishyate

(Chapter 3/7)

(*O Arjuna, he excels who restrains his senses by the mind, and undertakes selfless actions through sense organs without attachment.*)

This shloka commends the true spirit of inward detachment while strongly advocating the performance of actions through sense organs. The mind must keep senses under its control and then the organs of action must be used for desired outcomes. The Gita emphasizes the performance of all actions without any attachment or expectation. In simple language, this is what is called yoga or karmayoga in the Gita.

Shri Aurobindo succinctly explains this concept:

"Yoga is non-attachment to work and the results thereof. Yoga is not inaction, to mistake it for inaction is a grave confusion. True yoga is mindful, sincere actions without clinging to results."

It does not imply that one should not be attentive to the way an action is performed or be insensitive to its consequences. The message of the Gita is loud and clear that one should not be unduly obsessed with the acts being performed, nor get excessively perturbed if the results are adverse or less than expected.

The important message of the Gita is to understand that everybody loves to work and a leader should lead his organisation with this conviction. A leader should follow the precepts of yoga keeping his senses under control and remaining unattached to actions as well as their consequences.

Key Learnings

- Work is intrinsic to human nature and the driver of all civilization and cultural progress
- It is a prevalent belief in organisations that people are inherently lazy. This attitude creates an unfriendly and hostile environment leading to trust deficit.
- In a climate of mistrust no great goal can be achieved, however capable the leadership might be.

- The Gita offers a radically different and more positive perspective: that no one can remain idle, even for a moment.
- A leader must lead with the conviction that everyone naturally loves to work and should create an environment that nurtures this innate drive.

•••••

Success Mantra 2

Delegate with Discretion

Every significant assignment or work needs the sincere effort of people working together as a team. Not much can be achieved by an individual working alone. It is very important that the value of effective delegation is understood by leaders at the helm of affairs. The inability to delegate is one of the biggest problems in all organisations at all levels. No person who wants to do it all by himself or get all the credit will be able to achieve outstanding results.

The first principle of efficient management is delegation. One should not try to do everything oneself; it is simply not possible. Delegation is of critical importance for any organisation, but for bigger and complex entities, it is indispensable. However, it has to be based on due discretion and be the result of well thought out exercise.

Theodore Roosevelt aptly observed:

"The best executive is the one who has sense enough to pick good people to do what he wants done, and self-restraint enough to keep from meddling with them while they do it."

Ronald Reagan echoed the same wisdom: 'Surround yourself with the best people you can find, delegate authority, and don't interfere as long as the policy you've decided upon is being carried out.' Delegation of authority and allocation of responsibilities are matters that require great wisdom and judgement from any leader.

According to the Gita, there are three categories of people—*sattvik, rajasik* and *tamasik*—based on their basic instincts and nature. The characteristics of each of these personality types are described in detail in the Gita. It is very essential for a leader to study and properly understand the basic nature and leanings of his team in order to efficiently allocate different tasks and assignments to them.

Krishna, describing the qualities of sattvik people, says:

मुक्तसंगोऽनहंवादी धृत्युत्साहसमन्वितः।
सिद्धयसिद्ध्योर्निर्विकारः कर्ता सात्विक उच्यते।।

(अध्याय 18/26)

Muktasangonahamvaadi dhrtyutsaahasamanvitah
Siddhyasiddhyornirvikaarah kartaa saattvika uchyate

(Chapter 18/26)

(*Free from attachment and ego, steadfast, enthusiastic, and un-swayed by success or failure—such a doer is said to be sattvik.*)

Dispelling the general notion that people belonging to this category could be only involved in intellectual and spiritual pursuits, Krishna explains in the given shloka that sattvik people are not inactive; rather, they are full of enthusiasm and determination and perform their actions with equanimity. Such people have a sense of detachment towards worldly objects, are egoless and have great resolve to pursue their endeavours. Sattvik people, by their very nature, are not unduly influenced by success and failure, and are fully devoted to their duties.

According to some scholars, at least 10 per cent of the people in an organisation should be of sattvik nature, and these persons should be actively involved in setting organisational vision and goals. Such a group should be carefully identified and suitably empowered to suggest proper strategy for the growth and the direction of the organisation.

The next shloka of the Gita describes basic traits and attitudes of people belonging to the rajasik category:

रागी कर्मफलप्रेप्सुर्लुब्धो हिंसात्मकोऽशुचिः।
हर्षशोकान्वितः कर्ता राजसः परिकीर्तितः।।

(अध्याय 18/27)

Raagee karmaphalaprepsurlubdho hinsaatmakoshuchih
Harshashokaanvitah kartaa raajasah parikeertitah.

(Chapter 18/27)

(*The doer who is attached, craves the fruit of action, is greedy, violent, impure, and swayed by joy and sorrow has been called to be Rajasik.*)

Rajasik people are full of ambition, attachment and aggression, and are never satisfied with what they achieve. They are not bothered about purity of intentions or means being used in pursuit of their objectives, and are extremely sensitive to the success and failure of their endeavours. By virtue of their basic nature, they are able to achieve any objective that they set their eyes on, and are most suitable to pursue their goals.

However, being deeply passionate in their intent, actions and conduct, it is very important for a leader to put in place a proper mechanism to keep an eye and regulate their activities on a continuous basis. Keeping in view the characteristics of rajasik nature, about 40 per cent people should belong to this category in order to compete and overtake other organisations.

Finally, Krishna explains the Tamasik type:

अयुक्तः प्राकृतः स्तब्धः शठो नैष्कृतिकोऽलसः।
विषादी दीर्घसूत्री च कर्ता तामस उच्यते।।

(अध्याय 18/28)

Ayuktah praakritah stabdhah shatho naishkrtikolasah
Vishaadee deerghasootree cha kartaa taamasa uchyate

(Chapter 18/28)

(*The doer who is unsteady, uncultured, obstinate, deceitful, malicious, despondent, lazy, and a procrastinator is said to be tamasik.*)

According to the Gita, tamasik nature is nothing but lack of dash, drive and initiative, along with a dominance of dullness and apathy in the conduct of a person. Such people consider pleasure and comfort to be of paramount importance and are basically lazy and lethargic by nature. These people have closed their eyes, ears and even mind to reason and rationality. They are by temperament cunning, vile and vulgar, and are neither inclined nor capable of controlling their basic instincts of lust, pleasure and laziness. They have no initiative and are of procrastinating nature. They are generally fit for activities requiring labour and manual efforts. People of this category may be trained to be obedient and hardworking under effective leadership and strict supervision. It may be argued that in organisations where large numbers of employees are needed and the work primarily requires physical exertion, people of tamasik leanings may be accommodated.

It is important to note that individuals are rarely purely sattvik, rajasik or tamasik. It is difficult to place people in distinct categories mentioned in these shlokas as people are generally a combination of these three categories, however, usually one trait predominates. Leaders must keep in mind the dominant aspect of an individual's personality and accordingly allocate tasks to him.

Depending on sensitivity and importance of the assignment, the leader should choose a suitable person for best results. However, this is also true that an individual, because of his upbringing, education, exposure and experiences bears a distinct personality and can be judged and recognised for suitable delegation by leaders.

In this context, it is to be understood that the proportion of people having sattvik, rajasik, and tamasik nature in an organisation will depend on its aims and objectives, its technology and culture, and the society it operates in. The sectors using high degree of scientific knowledge, sophisticated technologies like information technology (IT), telecommunication, artificial intelligence, space and nuclear sciences, etc., will require a different mix as compared to manufacturing and services.

Therefore, leaders are required to use their discretion in identifying and selecting suitable people for delegation. The identified persons should not only have the required skills and training specific to the positions but also their attitudes, leanings and basic nature should match the requirement of the assignment.

The people entrusted with the responsibility of leading and formulating policies and strategies which affect vital aspects and large number of people in society should invariably have a dominant sattvik nature. Similarly, people working at the middle levels of hierarchy and responsible for implementing policies and programmes at the field level should have dominant rajasik elements in their personalities. Organisations having repetitive nature of duties with physical exertion and needing large number of people may find persons having predominantly tamasik nature suitable for the job. In such cases, proper training of people and strict supervision of their performance will have to be ensured.

Key Learnings

- Delegation is critical for organisational success: for large and complex organisations, it is indispensable.
- People, can broadly be classified into three categories—sattvik, rajasik and tamasik. – based on their basic nature.
- Sattvik individuals, marked by zeal, determination, and equanimity, are the most suited for tasks requiring vision, leadership, and steadfast execution.
- Rajasik people are action-oriented, ambitious and aggressive, and are able to achieve any objective that they set their eyes on.
- People of a tamasik nature lack dash, drive and initiative, and have dullness and apathy as dominant qualities.

- Leaders need to exercise due caution and use their best discretion while choosing people for delegation.

•••••

Success Mantra **3**

Act in Sync with Your Nature

The life of a human being is like a dense forest through which he must journey to reach his destination. The quality of his journey depends on many factors, such as his inherent nature, level of education, culture of the society he lives in, external environment, and most importantly, his personal vision for life.

Our success largely depends on our attitude towards work and the sincerity of our efforts.

Mark Twain once said:

> *"Do something every day that you don't want to do; this is the golden rule for acquiring the habit of doing your duty without pain."*

Thus, it is very essential for a human being to assess a viable option carefully and choose the right path.

Swami Vivekananda talked about the importance of focusing on one's own duties and even went on to say that devotion to duty is the highest form of worship.

The Gita says that the nature of duty and the resulting actions in different contexts are highly complex to understand. One should be able to clearly comprehend the difference between desirable action, inaction and undesirable action.

In common parlance, action means activities performed in the discharge of one's duty in a given situation. The proper understanding of one's duties is of paramount importance. Our success in life depends upon our understanding of these duties. A person acts according to his motives, the priorities he accords to specific actions and his views about expectations from such actions. Many times, the call of duty requires clarity regarding propriety, righteousness and relevance of a particular action in a given context. Sometimes our understanding about the need and significance of an action is not very obvious as the ensuing consequences may have much wider implications.

Choosing the right course of action in a complex situation is critical. Indian scriptures are a vast reservoir of wisdom and guidance. Their study and proper contemplation provide true guidance whenever we are confronted with dilemma while facing complicated situations in life. The Gita is one of the best reference scriptures to help us in choosing the right path.

Proper understanding of the issues and clarity about the right action in a complex situation is of great relevance.

Krishna says:

कर्मणो ह्यपि बोद्धव्यं बोद्धव्यं च विकर्मण: ।
अकर्मणश्च बोद्धव्यं गहना कर्मणो गति: ।।

(अध्याय 4 / 17)

Karmano hyapi boddhavyam boddhavyam cha vikarmanah.
Akarmanashcha boddhavayam gahanaa karmano gatih.

(Chapter 4/17)

(*One must understand the true nature of action, inaction and prohibited action, for mysterious are the ways of action.*)

Often, we encounter situations in life where it is quite difficult to distinguish between right and wrong actions. Many times, the traditions and social norms, inner voice, public expectations, and the exigencies of time and space can blur our judgment. In such situations, our wisdom and discernment become vital.

Mahatma Gandhi, writing in *Young India* revealed how he drew guidance from the Gita:

> *"When disappointment stares me in the face, and all alone, I see not a ray of light, I go back to the Bhagavad-Gita. I find a verse here and a verse there, and I immediately begin to smile in the midst of overwhelming tragedies. My life has been full of external tragedies, and if they have left no visible or indelible scar on me, I owe it all to the teachings of Bhagavad Gita. Those who meditate on the Gita will derive fresh joy and new meanings from it every day."*

The Gita strongly advocates focusing on one's own duty rather than getting attracted to the seemingly superior duties of others. Krishna tells Arjuna:

श्रेयान्स्वधमर्जो विगुणः परधर्मात्स्वनुष्ठितात्।
स्वधर्मे निधनं श्रेयः परधर्मो भयावहः।।

(अध्याय 3/35)

Shreyaansvadharmo vigunah paradharmaatsvanushthitaat.
Svadharme nidhanam shreyah paradharmo bhayaavahah.

(Chapter 3/35)

(*Better is one's own duty, though devoid of merit, than the well-performed duty of another. Even death in the course of performing one's own duty is blessed; performing another's duty is fraught with fear.*)

Krishna tells Arjuna that one should attend to one's own duties and never get lured to perform those of others, howsoever meritorious and beneficial they might appear.

The use of the word 'dharma' in the Gita does not stand for any religion, community, philosophy or ideology; instead, it primarily means one's prescribed duties and natural role in life. This point can be understood by the examples of a father's dharma—to love, care and provide for the children and family—and the dharma of a son—to obey and respect his father. Likewise, the dharma of the Sun is to radiate light and heat and that of a flower is to emanate fragrance all around. It is of utmost importance to properly understand one's dharma and conduct one's life accordingly.

Krishna reiterates this further:

श्रेयान्स्वधर्मो विगुण: परधर्मात्स्वनुष्ठितात् ।
स्वभावनियतं कर्म कुर्वन्नाप्नोति किल्बिषम् ।।

(अध्याय 18 / 47)

Shreyaansvadharmo vigunah paradharmaatsvanushthitaat.
Svabhaavaniyatam karma kurvannaapnoti kilbisham.

(Chapter 18/47)

(*It is better to do one's own dharma, though full of flaws, than another's dharma, well-performed. By performing one's own innate dharma, one does not incur sin.*)

Krishna exhorts Arjuna to fight the righteous war, reminding him that abstaining from it would be against his duties, training, his calling, and his true nature.

Dharma in the Gita refers to the path prescribed to each one according to one's own context and station in life. The duty of a teacher to teach sincerely, the duty of a student to listen attentively, and the duty of a leader to serve people honestly—all fall within the purview of their dharma, the prescribed duty for them. It is evident, therefore, that one must remain fully aware of one's dharma in its true essence and earnestly strive to act in accordance with it. This is much more important for a leader, as the team and other employees watch the leader and try to emulate him in every aspect of their conduct.

If we abandon our own dharma under someone else's influence, finding fault with it and adopting another's dharma, we act against our innate nature. An act performed under such conditions is ultimately not part of our own being, is external to it and has its own repercussions.

For successful functioning of an organization, various roles need to be assigned to different people depending on the nature of task, and their ability, training and experience. If people start neglecting their own duties by encroaching upon others' jurisdiction, great confusion and chaos will prevail. In any competent medical team, the tasks of a chief surgeon, assisting team of doctors, and other supporting medical staff including pre-operative and post-operative teams have to be distinct and well-defined for success of the operation. Any mixing of duties or confusion in the teams will have serious consequences for all concerned.

If we follow our dharma we act in tune with our innate nature, training and expertise which have been part of our growing, our own evolution. Such acts are quite inherent to our psyche, comfortable to our intellect and are performed efficiently, as a natural extension of our own persona, our own being. Therefore, it is in complete accordance with our innate nature.

Acting contrary to our true nature, however, leads to inner conflict, misery, and discontent.

Key Learnings

- A leader must clearly understand the difference between desirable action, inaction and undesirable action, for the nature of duty is very complex and needs clarity for success.
- The use of the word dharma in the Gita does not stand for any religion, community, philosophy or ideology; instead, it primarily means one's prescribed duties in life.
- One should focus upon performing one's own duties and never get lured to perform those of others.
- Following our dharma, we act in tune with our own nature, inclination and beliefs, which have been part of our growth and evolution.
- If we abandon our own dharma under external influences, we violate our innate nature which ultimately leads to confusion and suffering.

•••••

Success Mantra **4**

Your Right is to Work Only

The foremost responsibility of a leader is to inspire and motivate the team to work with competence, efficiency and dedication towards achieving shared goals. No organisation can rise to great heights without vigorous efforts of a highly motivated team working together on a sustained basis. In any institution, whether it is a family, corporate, political or social organisation, extraordinary results can never be achieved unless the leadership is able to motivate people to do their best.

In the great war of Mahabharata, as Arjuna reached the battlefield, he saw his gurus, uncles, grand- uncles, great grand-uncles, brothers, cousins, sons, nephews, friends and well-wishers in both the armies ready to fight the war. Seeing everyone ready to fight, Arjuna was overcome with great emotion and compassion and felt extremely depressed and confused. He described his vulnerable physical and emotional state to Krishna and cast aside his famous bow, the Gandiva, and his quill of arrows, and sat down in his chariot. He ascribed his hesitance to the presence of his relatives and elders on both sides. His limbs gave way, his bow slipped from his hands; he could not find a justification for the war and feared committing the sin of fighting and killing his own elders, gurus and kith and kin. Arjuna, shattered and agitated by grief and confusion, declared his resolve not to fight the war.

Seeing Arjuna crestfallen and totally disillusioned, Krishna decided to intervene and motivate him to rethink and correct his views in the light of his dharma and act accordingly. Krishna wanted to educate and enlighten Arjuna by imparting eternal wisdom and exhorting him to shed his despair and join the war that was being fought for truth and justice. That is how the Gita, a great repository of knowledge and action was bestowed upon the world and has provided guidance that continues to transform lives across the generations.

The sole aim was to motivate, educate and enlighten Arjuna, one of the greatest warriors of his time about the realities of life, his dharma and the obligation to follow it.

Krishna admonished Arjuna about his unexpected response in the midst of the armies on the battlefield:

कुतस्त्वा कश्मलमिदं विषमे समुपस्थितम्।
अनार्यजुष्टमस्वर्ग्यमकीर्तिकरमर्जुन।।

(अध्याय 2/2)

Kutastvaa kashmalamidam vishame samupasthitam
Anaaryajushtamasvargyamakeertikaramarjuna.

(Chapter 2/2)

(*Arjuna, how has this dejection overtaken you in this hour of crisis? It is not befitting of noble men. It will neither bring you heaven, nor fame.*)

It is observed that all of us, at some point in our lives, lose our enthusiasm and feel dejected and clueless. In such situations, inspiration and proper motivation by our elders or close friends work wonders and impart a renewed vigour to awaken and chart out a new roadmap to guide us.

It may be relevant to add that Arjuna didn't refuse to fight the war because of any principle or his understanding about the futility of war; his agitation was mainly the result of his attachment towards his elders, gurus and relatives who were standing right there in front of him on the battlefield. In fact, he became confused about having to fight his own kith and kin, and kill them. This sudden emotional state was the result of his confused view of life and lack of the larger perspective of the war. The war of Kurukshetra was the result of protracted animosity and conspiracy set in motion by Duryodhana and the failure of all efforts made to avoid the war, which was ultimately being fought by the Pandavas for truth and justice.

There is no other better example for motivating a dejected and disillusioned person than the case of Arjuna as given in the Gita. The teachings are most relevant for every situation in life. Arjuna, who initially refused to fight the war, ultimately understood the truth of life and his dharma after Krishna's prolonged discourse that finally took the form of the Gita.

Proper motivation based on sound logic and lofty objectives can transform the behaviour of the people and remain entrenched in their minds for long. But motivation based on vague and superficial reasoning does not have a lasting effect and has a limited impact in situations where sustained efforts are required to achieve desired goals. Effective motivation in an organisation should be based on sound principles and present a win-win situation for all stakeholders in a given context. If a leader is able to effectively motivate the members of their core team, the team will not only strive to perform their duties to the best of their abilities, but also act as catalysts, inspiring others to achieve the set goals.

To motivate Arjuna, Krishna propounds a unique work ethic in the following shloka:

कर्मण्येवाधिकारस्ते मा फलेषु कदाचन।
मा कर्मफलहेतुर्भूर्मा ते संगोऽस्त्वकर्मणि।।

(अध्याय 2/47)

Karmanyevaadhikaaraste maa phaleshu kadaachana.
Maa karmaphalaheturbhurma te sangostvakarmani.

(Chapter 2/47)

(*Your right is to work only and never to the fruits thereof. Do not consider yourself to be the cause of the fruit of action; nor let your attachment be to inaction.*)

According to many scholars, this extremely popular and oft-quoted shloka contains the central theme of the Gita. Krishna propounds an entirely new philosophy of action, which advocates performing one's duties without any sense of doership or attachment to the results. It advances a revolutionary work ethic, where one needs to perform his duties in a detached manner, without any desire for results; at the same time, one is exhorted never to be complacent and inclined towards inaction.

This shloka gives four important instructions regarding the science of action. Firstly, it reiterates that one has the right only to perform one's duties. Secondly, it affirms that one should not be concerned with the fruits of one's actions as they are beyond the doer. The third message is to shun the ego about one's 'doership'. The fourth and final instruction given in the shloka is to never be attached to inaction.

We only have the right to do our duty and perform our actions; the result, however, is not in our control. If we are concerned about the results of our actions, we will face undue anxiety and disappointment. Krishna, therefore, advises Arjuna not to bother about the results of his actions, and instead focus on performing his duties only.

Leaders need to be aware that actions performed without attachment will lead to desirable consequences, whereas actions based on self-interest and petty motives never lead to extraordinary results. There is great logic in this wisdom as actions performed with detachment eliminate undue concerns and worries. Similarly, actions performed without obsessive concern for results are better sustained and invariably lead to favourable consequences.

Action is an innate part of human nature and inevitable to sustain life. This shloka, therefore, is a 'mahamantra' for leaders tasked with motivating their team on a sustained basis. Actions performed without any sense of 'doership' or longing for results—especially on the part of a leader—enable him to create and sustain momentum in achieving the objectives of the organization. In the absence of feelings of 'doership', there is less possibility of conflict and envy in upper echelons of hierarchy, and consequently, a leader is free to plan and devise policies and programmes to achieve the ultimate objectives of the organisation. Similarly, if there is no obsessive concern for results, a leader is able to absorb the shocks of adverse developments in running an organisation, resort to midcourse corrections and sustain the momentum of onward journey towards its desired destination. Such efforts invariably lead to great success in achieving aims and objectives, maintaining the organisation's cohesiveness, and establishing inspiring legacies.

Key Learnings:

- The foremost responsibility of a leader is to inspire his team to work with competence, efficiency, and dedication towards shared goals.
- No organisation can rise to great heights without the sustained efforts of a highly motivated team working together.
- Effective leadership should be based on sound principles offering a win-win situation for all stakeholders.
- Being overly attached to results leads to undue anxiety and disappointment, as we only have control over our actions, not their outcomes.
- A leader must focus on his duties, free from ego and expectations, while never falling prey to inaction.

•••••

Success Mantra 5

Skillful Action is Yoga

The most important responsibility of a leader is to ensure the happiness and well-being of members of his team and the people he intends to serve through the organization. The happiness of every individual is of utmost importance for the growth and development of society. It is observed that in today's life, despite having the means of attaining comfort and security, people are not happy— they are dissatisfied with the government, the society, their employer or employees, and even with close family members. It makes us wonder the reasons behind this, and what can be done to change this scenario in the present context.

Today, with the availability of instant communication and access to endless information, people across the world are demanding a better quality of life, comfort and security. In such a situation, any gap in performance and expectations, real or perceived, leads to disharmony and chaos. This is a real challenge for leaders and managers in almost all organisations.

The development of the full potential of individuals has been a major objective as well as challenge since time immemorial, right from the benevolent kings, rishis and spiritual leaders to the political and business leaders of today. All scriptures in the world—the Vedas, Upanishads, the Mahabharata, the Gita, the Ramayana, the Bible, and the Quran—emphasise the importance of a person's inner development for a joyful and meaningful life.

Each individual is important for the evolution of a cultured and progressive society. It is always at an individual level that new visions and ideas emerge, which later become a trend or movement and give society a new direction of thinking, living and behaving. Human history is full of such visionary individuals who played great roles to transform society by their valuable contributions and made the world a much better place. The examples of Gautam Buddha, Mahavira, Christ and many others are there to learn from and emulate. Their vision, philosophy and conduct showed new paths to suffering humanity and ushered it into a new era.

Similarly, a large number of scientists, by their individual efforts in the last two centuries, have immensely contributed to the field of science, technology and medicine, thereby making the lives of people much more safe, comfortable and joyful. Taking the context of present times, Steve Jobs changed the entire concept of mobile technology and its usages, not only to make communication accessible to all but also revolutionizing the sector in terms of technology, efficiency and design. It has affected the quality of life for billions of people in innumerable ways. The new tools of social media have touched every aspect of human life and enhanced the ease, pace and comfort of people beyond recognition. It has affected social interaction, routine lifestyle, mode of relationships and has converted the world into a global village.

There is hardly any better example than the dialogue between Krishna and Arjuna in the Gita which initiated and facilitated the evolution of Arjuna from being a person full of anguish and delusion to taking the call of his duty and declaring in the end that he will fight the war. During the whole process of Krishna's discourse, Arjuna comes across as an honest and inquisitive individual who expresses his doubts, fears and frailties truthfully with the intent to learn and understand. He freely talks about his trembling limbs, burning skin, lack of balance and wavering mind, and seeks assistance and guidance. It is doubtful whether any other warrior of his stature would have mentioned his weakness and frailties in such a remarkably candid manner. Krishna, being his friend, philosopher and guide does his best to satisfy his queries and quell his fears and help him evolve through the prolonged discourse. Krishna's constant endeavour is to remove the doubts and dilemma from Arjuna's mind and help him realize his dharma in the right perspective.

In today's context, the challenges that people in leadership roles face are as complex, be it within the family, at work, or in the government. In the present scenario, one requires all the skills on his part to deftly handle challenges by taking the organisation along and addressing relevant concerns and interests.

This point has been beautifully articulated by Krishna in the following shloka:

बुद्धियुक्तो जहातीह उभे सुकृतदुष्कृते।
तस्माद्योगाय युज्यस्व योगः कर्मसु कौशलम्।।

(अध्याय 2/50)

Buddhiyukto jahaateeha ubhe sukritdushkrite.
Tasmaadyogaaya yujyasva yogah karmasu kaushalam.

(Chapter 2/50)

(*One whose intellect is established in equanimity sheds both good and evil in this very life. Therefore, strive for yoga; yoga is skill in action.*)

Krishna further enlightens Arjuna about the importance of balanced conduct and evenness of mind in confronting complexities of life. Achieving success in life requires mature decision-making and competent handling of emergent situations without getting deterred by problems and adversities.

In this process, Krishna tells Arjuna the importance of transcending the dualities of life and treating success and failure, as well as joy and sorrow, alike. He introduces the concept of yoga and says that yoga is nothing but the art of acting skillfully and treating ups and downs of life in a calm and detached manner. The skill in action is to develop an attitude of equanimity and treat joy and suffering alike without being affected by them.

However, practising equanimity is not easy. Arjuna, eager to understand further asks Krishna:

स्थितप्रज्ञस्य का भाषा समाधिस्थस्य केशव।
स्थितधीः किं प्रभाषेत किमासीत व्रजेत किम्।।

(अध्याय 2/54)

Sthitaprajnasya ka bhaashaa samaadhisthasya Keshava.
Sthitdheeh kim prabhaasheta kimaaseeta vrajeta kim.

(Chapter 2/54)

(*O Keshav! What is the disposition of one having stable mind and established in consciousness? How does one with a stable mind speak, how does he sit,how does he walk?*)

Arjuna asks to know the characteristics of a person who has attained a stable mind and wants to know the nature, his intellect and the manifestations of his conduct and behaviour. The conduct and behaviour of a person is said to be an expression of his thought process and innate nature. If one is calm and quiet, his ways of outward behaviour will be pleasant, steady and peaceful. But the behaviour of a person having an agitated mind will be unsteady and erratic. But these are the patterns of a normal human being, whereas the attributes under discussion are of a person who is established in consciousness, who is practicing yoga, the skill in action.

But Krishna rather than describing the external signs of such a person, describes the inner state:

प्रजहाति यदा कामान्सर्वान्पार्थ मनोगतान्।
आत्मन्येवात्मना तुष्टः स्थितप्रज्ञस्तदोच्यते।।

(अध्याय 2/55)

Prajahaati yadaa kaamaansarvanpaartha manogataan.
Aatmanyevaatmanaa tushtah sthitprajnastadochyate.

(Chapter 2/55)

(*Arjuna, when one discards all desires of the mind and becomes satisfied in the self alone, he is said to be of steady wisdom.*)

Krishna tells Arjuna that a person with a stable mind and balanced disposition always remains content in himself and is devoid of all desires. The real test is the discarding of all desires and inability of desires to affect the peace of mind. It is an inner state of freedom in which even if one is acting outwardly, he is fully within himself and external forces are not able to disturb his peace and calmness.

The previous shloka describes the inner state of a person with a stable mind and indicates that casting off all desires and being satisfied in one's own self are the most important characteristics of an evolved human being.

Krishna further clarifies the point in the following shloka:

या निशा सर्वभूतानां तस्यां जागर्ति संयमी।
यस्यां जाग्रति भूतानि सा निशा पश्यतो मुनेः।।

(अध्याय 2/69)

Yaa nishaa sarvabhutaanaam tasyaam jaagarti samyamee.
Yasyaam jaagrati bhutaani sa nishaa pashyato muneh.

(Chapter 2/69)

(*What is night for all beings is the time of waking for the disciplined soul; and the time of waking for all beings is the night for the sage of vision.*)

When all beings are charmed by material things, the one with a disciplined mind remains aloof and alert. He is not obsessed and lost in the material aspects of life. He is wakeful to the nature of reality whereas the unwise gets carried away and suffers the pain caused by the ways of life.

It is evident that to lead a life with purpose and meaning, alertness and awakening of one's inner being are very critical factors. The qualities of a stable mind and calm and composed disposition enable a person to handle adversities of life with an even temperament. A leader having such qualities can very easily inspire confidence in his team and lead it to exalted heights. The case of Mahatma Gandhi and his methods of truth and non-violence during the freedom struggle are shining examples to buttress this point and understand the eternal wisdom of the Gita.

Krishna, giving the example of an ocean, clarifies the above point to Arjuna:

आपूर्यमाणमचलप्रतिष्ठं
समुद्रमापः प्रविशन्ति यद्वत्।
तद्वत्कामा यं प्रविशन्ति सर्वे
स शान्तिमाप्नोति न कामकामी।।

(अध्याय 2/70)

Aapooryamaanamachalapratishtham
samudramaapah pravishanti yadvat.
Tadvatakaamaa yam pravishantisarve
sa shaantimaapnoti na kaamakaami.

(Chapter 2/70)

(*As the sea, though full on all sides, remains undisturbed even though countless rivers flow into it, so too does a person who is unmoved by desires attains peace; not he, who seeks to gratify desires.*)

Krishna says that a person who is not disturbed by material desires attains peace in the same manner as an ocean remains unaffected by water of different rivers entering it. But a person who is obsessed with material objects will never attain peace. Only a person in control of his desires can lead a perfect life as mundane happenings of life—success and failure, and zest and despair—are not able to affect the calmness of his mind. Similarly, a person in position of authority needs to develop a balanced disposition and take sunny days and rainy season both in his stride without getting disturbed in his mind. To run a long race, one has to transcend the feelings of joy as well as despair, and continue his efforts to reach the ultimate destination. This is possible only when one has mastered the art of self-discipline, is content within himself and is unaffected by countless desires visiting his mind.

In the context of normal conduct of life, to achieve the above state of mind and be totally devoid of desire is not possible but the wisdom contained in the above shlokas suggests that one should neither be overjoyed and loose discretion in moments of success nor be engulfed by despair and act under depression when confronted with loss or failure. A leader will have to meet many ups and downs in implementation of various policies and decisions in his carrier but the wisdom of the Gita says that instead of getting carried away with success or deflecting from the path in the event of failure, he should reconsider the options and consequences with a cool mind, revise suitably and sustain the momentum to achieve the intended results and consequences. The Gita has provided guidance to people through generations both in moments of success and failure and inspired them to continue the onward journey with grit and enthusiasm.

Key Learnings

- The priority of a leader should be to improve the quality of life and enhance the happiness of his people.
- Yoga is skill in action—the art of transcending the dualities of life and treating success and failure alike.

- A person with a stable mind and balanced disposition remains satisfied within himself and is free from desires and cravings.
- One, who is not obsessed by material desires, attains peace in the same manner as an ocean remains unaffected by water of different rivers entering it.
- Only a person in control of his desires can lead a perfect life, remaining unaffected by the ups and downs of worldly experiences.

•••••

Success Mantra **6**

Blaze a Trail

The backdrop of the Gita is the battlefield of Kurukshetra where mighty armies had assembled for war. Yet, its teachings transcend the immediate context and remain profoundly relevant even today. The teachings contained within the text are equally relevant for people willing to live a purposeful life as well as those responsible for running an organization. The situations people face today are quite similar to what Arjuna faced on the battlefield. He came to the battlefield with the resolve to fight and ensure victory for his side but standing between both the armies he felt dejected, shattered and demotivated.

In the modern world, 'struggle for existence' and 'survival of the fittest' have become dominant mantra for life. Intense competition, rampant consumerism and a growing deficit of love, compassion and tolerance have led to widespread stress, anxiety, and suffering. In such a situation, the wisdom of the Gita appears to be extremely relevant and critical for peace, harmony and happiness. The intent and contents of the text are primarily aimed at guiding, motivating and inspiring human beings to engage in the battle of life with vigour and tenacity, without being perturbed and getting lost in the game of life.

Every person, at some point in his life, finds himself at a crossroads and faces a dilemma regarding the next course of action. The teachings of the Gita provide great refuge and a ray of hope even in the most dark and depressing situations. Krishna explained the concepts of immortality of the soul, inevitability of the cycle of birth and death, nature of dharma and paths of knowledge and action to Arjuna to correct his perspective and give him clarity about his dharma. He also emphasized the importance of attending to one's dharma and treating joy and sorrow alike.

Faced with inner turmoil, Arjuna sought further clarity from Krishna. Though Krishna had elaborated the paths of knowledge and action, Arjuna perplexed by the apparent contradiction, questioned:

ज्यायसी चेत्कर्मणस्ते मता बुद्धिर्जनार्दन
तत्किं कर्मणि घोरे मां नियोजयसि केशव।

(अध्याय 3/1)

Jyaayasee chetkarmanaste mataa buddhirjanaardana
Tatkim karmani ghore maam niyojayasi keshava.

(Chapter 3/1)

(O Krishna! If you consider knowledge as superior to action, why then do you urge me to engage in this dreadful action?)

व्यामिश्रेणेव वाक्येन बुद्धिं मोहयसीव मे
तदेकं वद निश्चित्य येन श्रेयोऽहमाप्नुयाम्।

(अध्याय 3/2)

Vyaamisheneva vaakyena buddhim mohayaseeva me
Tadekam vada nishchatya yen shreyohamaapnuyaam.

(Chapter 3/2)

(*You confuse my intellect with these seemingly conflicting versions. Therefore, tell me decisively the one path by which I may attain the highest good.*)

Arjuna wanted clarity between the paths of knowledge (*gnan* or sankhya yoga) and action (karma yoga or yoga) and asked that if Krishna considered the first one to be superior, then why was he urging him to do this savage deed. Finally, he asked Krishna to suggest an appropriate path which may be good for him. He points to the contradictory and confusing doctrines mentioned by Krishna, which though explained the concepts of both paths but didn't advise any specific path at this stage

Arjuna's questions appear to be organic to the pattern of dialogue already established in the light of reasons explained by Arjuna for laying down his arms and resolving not to fight. Now, having understood the perspective and context to some extent, Arjuna comes to a state where he asks for a specific path that is most appropriate and suitable for him.

At this critical juncture, Krishna addresses Arjuna's confusion advising him to perform his prescribed duty without hesitation.

नियतं कुरु कर्म त्वं कर्म ज्यायो ह्यकर्मणः।
शरीरयात्रापि च ते न प्रसिद्धयेदकर्मणः।।

(अध्याय 3/8)

Niyatam kuru karma tvam karma jyaayo hyakarmanah.
Shareerayaatraapi cha te na prasiddhyedakarmanah.

(Chapter 3/8)

(*Perform your prescribed duty, for action is superior to inaction. Without action, even the maintenance of your physical life would be impossible.*)

Krishna strongly advocates the virtue of performing one's duties according to one's station in life. He further says that if a person stops carrying out his responsibilities, he cannot even maintain his own body. This is very sound logic as inaction leads us nowhere. We have seen that action is innate to human nature and one cannot remain for even a moment without indulging in some action. Action is the only route through which we can elevate our mind and intellect.

Therefore, Krishna asks Arjuna to perform his prescribed duties, as it is the only honourable option in human life. It is important in every situation—be it family, organisation or society—that everyone performs his given duty as life is interdependent on one another. A family cannot lead a purposeful life if parents don't fulfill their obligations to take care of their children, protect and provide for them. So is true for every organisation. No organisation can function properly and meet its obligations unless the leaders and managers working at the helm of affairs take decisions and provide appropriate guidance.

Another important principle enunciated by Krishna in the Gita is to perform one's action with a sense of non-attachment. A person who performs his actions with attachment and is obsessed with results creates bondage for himself. He will never experience freedom and will ever remain trapped in the whirlpools of longings and sufferings. This point is further clarified by Krishna in the following shloka:

तस्मादसक्तः सततं कार्यं कर्म समाचर।
असक्तो ह्याचरन्कर्म परमाप्नोति पूरुषः।।

(अध्याय 3/19)

Tasmaadasaktah satatam kaaryam karma samaachara.
Asakto hyaacharankarma paramaapnoti poorushah.

(Chapter 3/19)

(*Therefore, always perform your duty without attachment; for man attains the highest by performing actions without attachment.*)

The duty described in the Gita consists of actions integral to the innate nature of a person and expected of him due to his position in life. It is primarily called dharma in the Gita.

The Gita highlights the importance of performing actions with a sense of detachment in the conduct of actions as well as their consequences. It is a unique philosophy which Krishna in the Gita advocates as a code of conduct for every human being. It is difficult to presume the ways of life where deeds are performed in total absence of attachment with the action as well as its results. But the

Gita envisages performance of actions with due diligence and efficiency without clinging to the acts and bothering about the results of actions. The main idea behind this philosophy is that lack of attachment with the acts as well as the results provides great freedom and avoids the sense of bondage which otherwise is the inevitable consequence and cause of sorrows and sufferings.

The practice of this principle in the conduct of one's life is very much possible and as the previous shloka suggests, by performing one's duty with detachment, one can attain the highest in material as well as spiritual life. There are innumerable examples of sages and saints, benevolent kings, leaders and spiritual persons who performed their duties in full earnestness but were devoid of attachment to their chores, kingdoms or any kind of self-interests as well as the results and consequences following their acts. Such people attained the highest in their chosen fields and provided right guidance and inspiration to mankind. History is full of such names right from Buddha, Mahavira, Christ, Gandhi, Ram Krishna Paramhansa, Paramahansa Yogananda and many others.

The Gita itself gives the example of King Janaka who reached perfection and attained the supreme through action without attachment. Janaka was the king of Mithila and father of Sita, the wife of Rama, who ruled and attended to all his worldly duties as a king without any attachment or entertaining the sense of being a doer. He was fully convinced that these are the senses which are engaged in the activities.

Krishna further underscores the critical role of leaders through this timeless verse:

यद्यदाचरति श्रेष्ठस्तत्तदेवेतरो जनः।
स यत्प्रमाणं कुरुते लोकस्तदनुवर्तते।।

(अध्याय 3/21)

yadyadaacharati shreshthastattadevetaro janah sa
yatpramanam kurute lokastadanuvartate

(Chapter 3/21)

(Whatever a great man does, others follow. Whatever standard he sets, the world pursues.)

The Gita points out that a great man who works with no selfish motive and performs his actions without attachments is the one who blazes a trail that others willingly follow. Such a person is way ahead of society and can be called a true leader in the real sense of the term. This is a great message of the Gita and following it one can make his life a profound success both in material as well as spiritual aspects.

In today's societal context, leaders bear a moral responsibility to serve the people with detachment and to inspire them through the force of their personal thoughts, words, and actions. When such enlightened leaders stand at the forefront, society naturally follows, enabling transformational change in social conduct and collective growth. This, in turn, fosters deeper relationships and contributes to lasting joy and happiness for all. History offers numerous examples of such leaders—individuals like Lincoln, Gandhi, Mandela, and many other heroic figures—who illuminated new paths for humanity through their selfless actions and noble sacrifices.

Key Learnings

- In today's world, the 'struggle for existence' and 'survival of the fittest' dominate the pursuit of success.
- The Gita's teachings are invaluable when faced with doubts and dilemma about the right course of action.
- Duty in the Gita refers to actions aligned with one's innate nature and responsibilities as per one's station in life.
- A leader should perform his duty without attachment as it sets an inspiring example for society.

- A true leader should blaze a trail because whatever a great man does, others follow.

•••••

Success Mantra 7

Motivation: An Art of Inspiring

Motivation is the art of inspiring people to do what one wants them to do. It is an act of exercising influence over the conduct and response of others through thoughts, words or actions.

Motivation includes the efforts of a person normally in the position of authority or leadership to influence attitude, beliefs, thoughts, notions and impressions, and eventually expecting a person or a group to do the needful to the best of their potential. To inspire a person to realise his own potential and do his best to achieve his own goals and objectives is also motivation. The idea behind the concept of motivation is that human beings are rational and their behaviour can be influenced by thoughts, words and actions.

Motivation can be self-driven or externally influenced. Self-driven motivation is the desire to express oneself through one's own acts and take up new challenges. It is to do something new on one's own initiative, without any external stimuli. It is caused by an interest or joy in the task itself and does not depend upon any reward or recognition from external forces. Self-driven motivation is generally long-lasting and self-sustaining. For such motivation, one gets the drive from within and the strength and sustenance from his own belief, ambition and philosophy of life.

External motivation, as the name suggests, is the opposite of self-driven motivation and it comes from outside the individual from another source. Motivation used by leaders falls in this category and is aimed at achieving desired outcomes by making people share the aims and objectives of the organization and work for it.

The main task of a leader is to motivate people to ensure a predetermined response on a sustained basis. It is by no means an easy task. To motivate, a leader needs to touch some deep chord in the psyche of the people and affect their thoughts and beliefs to elicit their support in achieving organisational goals.

During the long discourse of the Gita, Krishna uses various arguments to motivate Arjuna to transform his viewpoint and make him understand the reality of his situation and his role in it. He tried to change his emotional perceptions about the war even by reprimanding him and using strongly worded arguments. Krishna called his response and refusal to wage the war as untimely, unprecedented, unworthy of a warrior, heaven-denying, and sure to bring ill-repute.

Probably Krishna could not be more direct and hard-hitting:

क्लैब्यं मा स्म गमः पार्थ नैतत्त्वय्युपपद्यते।
क्षुद्रं हृदयदौर्बल्यं त्यक्त्वोत्तिष्ठ परंतप।।

(अध्याय 2/3)

Klaibyam maa sma gamah Paartha naitattvayyupapadyate.
Kshudram hridayadaurbalyam tyaktvottishtha parantapa.

(Chapter 2/3)

(O Arjuna, do not yield to unmanliness. It does not become you. Renounce this paltry faint-heartedness and arise, O oppressor of foes.)

Krishna admonished Arjuna for his unexpected weakness of heart and further reminded him that this response was not worthy of a warrior like him. In this shloka, he calls upon Arjuna to understand his duty and stand up to fight.

Arjuna, being a great warrior and a determined person of proven tenacity, was also firm in his convictions. He gave varied arguments in favour of his decision to desist from the war. Fame, glory, heaven or kingdom—nothing in his view justified the war and killing his gurus, elders and kinsmen. At this stage, he was not motivated to act even after being reprimanded by Krishna.

Arjuna responded in no uncertain words giving his own reason for his refusal:

गुरुनहत्वा हि महानुभावान्
श्रेयो भोक्तुं भैक्ष्यमपीह लोके।
हत्वार्थकामांस्तु गुरुनिहैव
भुन्जीय भोगान् रुधिरप्रदिग्धान्।।

(अध्याय 2/5)

Guroonahatvaa hi mahaanubhaavaan
Shreyo bhoktum bhaikshyamapeeha loke.

Hatvaarthakaamaamstu guroonihaiva
Bhunjeeya bhogaan rudhirpradigdhaan.

(Chapter 2/5)

(*It is better to live in this world on alms than slay these honoured teachers. Slaying them, I would be reveling in bloodstained pleasures of wealth and desire.*)

Arjuna told Krishna that killing his teachers would get him nothing but a bloodstained kingdom, which would not be worth it. Indicating the inevitable end of the war, he spoke about the futility and impropriety of it all.

The Gita is a very appropriate scripture to understand the complexities and intricacies in motivating people against their firm convictions. Even a skilful guru like Krishna found it difficult to motivate Arjuna to see things in the right perspective.

Krishna, advancing his arguments, asks Arjuna not to grieve for the inevitable:

अशोच्यानन्वशोचस्त्वं प्रज्ञावादांश्च भाषसे।
गतासूनगतासूंश्च नानुशोचन्ति पण्डिताः।।

(अध्याय 2/11)

Ashochyaananvasochastvam prajnaavaadaams cha bhaasase
Gataasoonagataasoonscha naanushochanti panditaah

(Chapter 2/11)

(*You grieve for those who should not be grieved for, and yet speak like a learned person. The wise grieve neither for the dead nor the living.*)

Krishna gradually advances and elevates the levels of conversation with the objective to affect Arjuna's thought process and mindset. He tries to change the direction of discussions and take Arjuna to a different level of consciousness.

Krishna tells him that though he is speaking like a learned person, his arguments are born of confusion and ignorance. These reasons in no way justify his grieving and resolve not to fight the war. The wise never lament for the living or the dead as it is an inevitable part of the cycle of life.

Krishna, continuing his effort to affect the attitude of Arjuna, tries to enlighten him about the basic truths of life. Keeping in view the issues raised by Arjuna while refusing to wage the war, Krishna tells him to take life's joy and sorrow in his stride without getting unduly obsessed with the outcomes.

Further Krishna encourages Arjuna to maintain equanimity in all circumstances:

सुखदुःखे समे कृत्वा लाभालाभौ जयाजयौ।
ततो युद्धाय युज्यस्व नैवं पापमवाप्स्यसि।।

(अध्याय 2/38)

Sukhaduhkhe same kritvaa laabhaalaabhau jayaajayau.
Tato yuddhaaya yujyasva naivam paapamavaapsyasi.

(Chapter 2/38)

(*Treat pleasure and pain, gain and loss, victory and defeat alike, and prepare for battle. Thus, you shall not incur sin.*)

Krishna calls upon Arjuna to exercise equanimity in joy and grief, gain and loss, victory and defeat—all dualities of life—and engage in the war. He further assures Arjuna that by doing so, he will not incur sin.

Success and failure are inevitable in the life of an individual or an organisation. A true leader has to be ready for the same and prepare his people for any kind of eventuality. The ways and means of motivation vary according to contexts and the organisations. The techniques followed by teachers in educational institutions will differ from the techniques to manage a large company or command a uniformed force.

A great leader needs to assess sensibilities, challenges and the preparedness of his organization in order to get best results. In a country like India, which has a large number of ethnic groups, cultural traditions, languages, ethos and beliefs, and the aspirations of a modern society, leaders and managers have to equip themselves well. They have to be sensitive to tangible and intangible factors in order to elicit proper responses and lead their organizations to the desired results.

The teachings of the Gita are the best example of motivation as all the factors regarding Arjuna's grief and confusion were dealt with in detail by Krishna in his long dialogue with Arjuna. It was not an easy task. Krishna tried to motivate him keeping in view his reputation as a warrior, the context of war, true philosophy of life, empathy and support from the motivator, tried to enlighten him in an imaginative, truthful and organic manner. In the end, his teachings enabled him achieve clarity of vision, right perspective and his questioning in the given situation.

Therefore, it is important for a motivator to be aware of the strength and weaknesses, sensibilities, previous experiences and track record challenges and aspirations of the people being motivated.

Key Learnings

- Motivation is the art of inspiring people and influencing their conduct and responses through thoughts, words or actions.

- It involves efforts to influence attitudes, beliefs, thoughts and impressions, leading to desired results.
- The primary responsibility of a leader is to ensure a predetermined response on a sustained basis through effective motivation.
- To motivate successfully, a leader must connect with the deeper layers of human psyche, influencing thoughts and beliefs.
- The methods of motivation vary according to the context – the techniques followed in educational institutions, employees, or soldiers differ significantly.
- Success and failure being inevitable in the life of an individual or an organisation; a true leader prepares his people to face both with resilience and equanimity.

•••••

Success Mantra **8**

Elevate Yourself

The central theme of the Gita is to inspire individuals to perform their duties without attachment to actions or their outcomes. This is very profound wisdom and has many far-reaching consequences. During the long discourse of the Gita, Arjuna is exposed to an entirely new worldview and finally experiences a new awakening. Up to the Kurukshetra war, he had faced many difficulties, won many battles and had established himself as a great archer and outstanding warrior. But his conduct right at the beginning of the war was entirely bewildering and against the very nature of a warrior like him.

Krishna explains to him the various aspects of action and asks him to understand the nature of action but never take recourse to inaction. Performing actions without attachment to the conduct or its consequences is in itself a new concept, where one is required to have no attachment with action as well as its results. In such a situation, performing an action acquires a new dimension with no strings attached before or after it. It needs firm resolve and clear understanding about the nature of action itself.

The concept of non-attachment reverberates throughout the Gita as Krishna tries to make Arjuna understand the importance of doing one's duty with complete dispassion. However, this is easier said than done.

Krishna further elaborates this point in one of the most inspiring shlokas of the Gita:

उद्धरेदात्मनाऽऽत्मानं नात्मानमवसादयेत्।
आत्मैव ह्यात्मनो बन्धुरात्मैव रिपुरात्मनः।।

(अध्याय 6/5)

Uddharedaatmanaatmaanam naatmaanamavasaadayet.
Aatmaiva hyaatmano bandhuraatmaiva ripuraatmanah.

(Chapter 6/5)

(*One should elevate oneself by one's own efforts and not degrade oneself; for one alone is the friend as well as the enemy of oneself.*)

This shloka explains the eternal truth that every man is his own friend as well as his own enemy, for it is our thoughts and actions that decide the destiny of our lives. It is entirely within us to elevate or degrade ourselves. It is observed that most of the time, our life is conducted based on our likes and dislikes and we remain unaware of the divine nature of the soul. To elevate ourselves requires us to control our desires, connect with the divine within, and realise the transitory nature of life, its true objectives and immense possibilities for our growth and evolution.

The real purpose is to lead a divine life and transcend the mundane aspects. Once we are able to control our impulses and connect with the higher self, we are able to understand the realities of life in the right perspective. Our future is in our hands, we have the freedom to rise or fall, to elevate or degrade ourselves.

Krishna asks Arjuna to elevate himself and not be trapped by material longings. He encourages him to understand the truth of human existence.

It is the prime duty of everybody to understand the myth of worldly existence and truth of eternal values of life to make life divine and meaningful. Life's journey is fraught with traps and distractions, and to keep it on the right track, one has to be extra alert to avoid the pitfalls and constantly watch and control one's desires.

Krishna further explains the ways one can achieve this:

तस्मात्त्वमिन्द्रियाण्यादौ नियम्य भरतर्षभ ।
पाप्मानं प्रजहि ह्येनं ज्ञानविज्ञाननाशनम् ।।

(अध्याय 3/41)

Tasmaattvamindriyaanyaadau niyamya Bharatarshabha
Paapmaanam prajahi hyenam jnaanavijnaanaashanam.

(Chapter 3/41)

(*Therefore, Arjuna, first control your senses and kill this sinful destroyer of knowledge and wisdom.*)

The faculties of knowledge and discernment are clouded by desires—the eternal enemy of the wise. A person under the spell of senses and their cravings is oblivious of the divinity of life and its immense possibilities. The Gita cites the examples of smoke covering the real nature and truth of fire and also of dirt which adversely impacts the viewing of a mirror to explain the effect of desires in polluting the mind and vision of a man. How to avoid the traps of desire and control it has been a great concern for saints and sages since ages. Krishna also enlightens Arjuna throughout the

Gita about the havoc uncontrolled desires can cause, and the need to control them.

According to the Gita, desire is the main root of evil and suffering, and therefore we must guard against the free run of the senses and the unhindered thirst of desires.

The power to control desires and elevate ourselves lies entirely within us. Krishna beautifully explains the hierarchy of consciousness:

इन्द्रियाणि पराण्याहुरिन्द्रियेभ्यः परं मनः।
मनसस्तु परा बुद्धिर्यो बुद्धेः परतस्तु सः।।

(अध्याय 3/42)

Indriyaani paraanyaahurindriyebhyah param manah
Manasastu paraa buddhiryo buddheh paratastu sah.

(Chapter 3/42)

(*The senses are superior to the body, the mind is superior to the senses, the intellect is superior to the mind, and the soul is superior to the intellect.*)

We should not be subservient to the diktats of our senses which keep us entrapped in the web of taste, touch, sight, smell and sound. We must realise the power of the mind over the senses. Therefore, the senses should not be permitted to dominate life's affairs through a captivating lure of lust and desire. The mind should exercise due caution and control on the senses. Krishna further says that the mind, being of a wavering nature, should be controlled by the intellect, and the intellect in turn should be guided by the awareness of the 'self', the inner wisdom that is a part of the universal consciousness. This is a very important shloka as it gives us a hierarchy of the levels of consciousness. The realisation of this hierarchy and its conscious practice gives us tremendous power to control the senses by exercising due caution and wisdom through mind. The wavering nature of mind can be controlled through intellect which derives its awareness from the 'self'.

This consciousness must be awakened step by step through practice and dispassion. The higher we rise, the more freedom we enjoy, because actions performed under the influence of the senses create their own chain of bondage and suffering. As we continue acting according to the diktats of the mind duly guided by the intellect, the degree of freedom is enhanced. We attain the highest state when our acts are fully determined by the intellect deriving its awareness from the ultimate divine source.

Krishna further asks Arjuna to understand the ways of desire and extinguish its fire:

एवं बुद्धेः परं बुद्ध्वा संस्तभ्यात्मानमात्मना।
जहि शत्रुं महाबाहो कामरूपं दुरासदम्।।

(अध्याय 3/43)

Evam buddheh param buddhvaa
sanstabhyaatmaanamaatmanaa
Jahi shatrum mahaabaaho kaamaroopam duraasadam.

(Chapter 3/43)

(*Thus, knowing the 'self' to be superior to the intellect, control the mind with the self. O mighty armed, destroy the formidable enemy called desire.*)

This powerful shloka advises that one must control the senses, mind and intellect through the awakened self, which derives its power and wisdom from the universal consciousness. This shloka provides an insight into the working of mind, intellect and soul and highlights the role of an awakened and enlightened soul. Such a soul controls and guides the senses exercising restraint through intellect and mind and thus regulates the free run of the senses and their indulgences. Acting in accordance with the above wisdom, one can lead a virtuous and purposeful life and avoid the traps of sense objects and baser instincts.

It is said that the wisdom of a human being is covered with ignorance and he is unaware of his immense potential. As a result, more often than not, he succumbs to the diktats of his desires and cravings ignited by the senses. If he realises his true potential and derives strength and guidance from his 'self', he can transcend any limitation and lead a life of freedom and awakening.

If we are not able to control the nefarious games of the mind and exercise control through intellect, desires will run amuck and dominate our mind. Consequently, life will get muddled and lost in the darkness of delusion and ignorance.

Therefore, Krishna asks Arjuna to subdue the desires ignited by senses through an aware mind duly guided by intellect that derives its light and inspiration from one's self.

The idea behind the above sequence of control is that an awakened soul will always remain alert and watchful to guide the intellect in the proper direction. In such a situation, the intellect is able to exercise due restraint and control over the senses through its wisdom and counsel imparted to the mind.

We need to understand the prime role of the 'self' to ensure righteous interplay of the intellect and the mind, in order to restrain the free run of senses and their unchecked indulgences in sense objects and material pleasures. It is the wavering mind and its raw, unhindered and unregulated desires that cloud the wisdom and the intellect, and cause great sorrows and suffering in human life. History is replete with innumerable examples of not only common people, kings and eminent leaders but also large number of sages and saints.

Key Learnings

- Each person is his own friend as well as own enemy; our thoughts and actions decide the destiny of our lives.
- The true purpose of life is to lead a meaningful life by transcending mundane and material distractions.
- We should not be subservient to the diktats of our senses which keep us entrapped in the web of taste, touch, sight, smell and sound.
- Desires born of the senses cloud our vision and impel us to run after material things which ultimately lead to lust, anger and greed.
- According to the Gita, desires can be subdued by a vigilant mind, an enlightened intellect, and a soul awakened to its divine essence.

•••••

Success Mantra **9**

A Lamp in a Windless Place Never Flickers

In the course of life's affairs, we often encounter complex and challenging situations that demand undivided attention and thoughtful reflections. Focused thinking is essential to tackle such problems and arrive at appropriate solutions. It is an accepted fact that the basic nature of the mind is to waver and entertain innumerable thoughts.

According to Patanjali, the father of the discipline of yoga, it is the very nature of the mind to incessantly pervade the realms of wandering, forgetting, distraction, focus and restraint but never settling down. When we are not able to focus, and our mind wavers, we face doubts and delusions. A restless and agitated mind is always occupied with various thoughts and countless issues. In such a condition, there is hardly any possibility to concentrate on the emergent issues and reach a prudent decision. Therefore, proper focus is vital to address critical situations and take sound decisions.

This is exactly what happened on the battlefield of Kurukshetra, when Arjuna lost his focus and found himself in a state of great delusion and dilemma. Being in a highly unstable state of mind and unable to focus on the task at hand, Arjuna failed to decide upon the right course of action, which was to fight and lead the Pandavas to victory in the battle. Instead, he decided to throw down his arms.

It happens in life that quite often one finds himself in difficult and overwhelming situations with no clear options in hand. Such situations require focused thoughts and the weighing of all pros and cons, but more often than not one is never at peace with himself to think through and take a cool-headed decision. In such situations, the greatest challenge is to keep one's cool, focus on the issue and take a call.

The Gita offers the art and science of 'minding' one's mind by treating the dualities of life with equanimity:

जितात्मनः प्रशान्तस्य परमात्मा समाहितः।
शीतोष्णसुखदुःखेषु तथा मानापमानयोः।।

(अध्याय 6/7)

Jitaatmanah prashaantasya paramaatmaa samaahitah.
Shitoshnasukhaduhkheshu tathaa maanaapamaanayoh.

(Chapter 6/7)

(*One who has conquered the self, attained perfect calmness and whose mind is perfectly calm and steady in the self, treats cold and heat, pleasure and pain, honour and dishonour alike.*)

Krishna emphasises the significance of being in full control of one's 'self' and thus exercise restraint on the senses through an alert mind and enlightened intellect. He tells Arjuna that in order to obtain the ability of transcending the dualities of life, one has to conquer his 'self' and be in constant union with the universal consciousness. The Gita very clearly elaborates that the contact of the senses with material objects creates dualities and is the root cause of pain and suffering. A self-realised person having control over his intellect, mind and senses never gets caught up in the dualities of pleasure and pain, heat and cold and honour and dishonour. He is able to see through these fleeting perceptions of human existence and remain unaffected and unmoved.

It is an accepted fact that a problem cannot be solved at the level at which it was created; to find solution, one must elevate one's understanding and see the situation with greater clarity and detachment. In any position of responsibility, one must interact with others, understand different viewpoints, and seek their support and cooperation to achieve meaningful objectives.

In a role of leadership, one has to understand the emotions and thoughts of people working at various levels in an organisation. A leader has also to watch his own thoughts and be alert and aware in processing the responses of his colleagues and workers. He should not be in an agitated state of mind and never get swayed by extraneous considerations or unchecked feedbacks. He should be in full control of himself while taking a call that impacts vital issues and large number of people.

Krishna beautifully illustrates the mental state of such a leader:

यथादीपो निवातस्थो नेंगते सोपमा स्मृता।
योगिनो यतचित्तस्य युंजतो योगमात्मनः।।

(अध्याय 6/19)

Yathaadeepo nivaatastho nengate sopamaa smritaa.
Yogino yatachittasya yunjato yogamaatmanah.

(Chapter 6/19)

(Just as a lamp in a windless place does not flicker, so is the state of a yogi's disciplined mind, absorbed in the state of yoga.)

The mind being fickle in nature is never stable and focused but the mind of a yogi being in constant communion with the universal self becomes steady and peaceful. According to the Gita, the mind of a person who practices the disciplining of his 'self' remains calm and steady, just like the wick of a lamp kept in a windless place.

Maintaining one's peace and calm, even in troubled situations, is one of the most important challenges of human life. Saints, sages, and scriptures across the world have acknowledged the enormous difficulty of keeping the mind calm and quiet, offering diverse methods to achieve it. The Gita addresses this challenge in great detail.

Acknowledging the difficulty, Arjuna confesses to Krishna:

चंचलं हि मनः कृष्ण प्रमाथि बलवद्दृढम्।
तस्याहं निग्रहं मन्ये वायोरिव सुदुष्करम्।।

(अध्याय 6/34)

Chanchalam hi manah Krishna pramaathi balavaddridham.
Tasyaaham nigraham manye vaayoriv sudushkaram.

(Chapter 6/34)

(*For the mind is very restless, O Krishna! It is turbulent, powerful and obstinate. I think it is as difficult to control as the wind.*)

Arjuna speaks about the restless, vehement and turbulent nature of the mind, and tells Krishna that the mind, in his view, is as hard to control as the wind. This is something we all will agree with. The restlessness of the mind is a common experience; it goes on flitting from one subject to another. It has been called turbulent because it gives rise to a variety of emotions that lead to lust, greed, envy, anger and fear, which adversely affect the calmness of the mind. The mind is said to be strong, as it overpowers the intellect and discretion and blurs one's vision and clarity. It is said to be obstinate because once it clings to a thought or craving, it's almost impossible to deflect it off its course.

Throughout human history, the agitation of the mind has caused innumerable upheavals and led to countless disasters at both individual and collective levels. It's difficult to disagree with the above description of the human mind. The beauty of the Gita's teachings is that it provides a clear solution to almost all human problems.

Krishna first acknowledges the problem one faces in controlling the mind and provides a solution:

असंशयं महाबाहो मनो दुर्निग्रहं चलम्।
अभ्यासेन तु कौन्तेय वैराग्येण च गृह्यते।।

(अध्याय 6/35)

Asamshayam mahaabaaho mano durnigraham chalam.
Abhyaasena tu Kaunteya vairaagyena cha grihyate.

(Chapter 6/35)

(O Mighty armed son of Kunti, undoubtedly the mind is restless and difficult to restrain; but it can be controlled through constant practice and detachment.)

Krishna accepts that the mind is restless and difficult to restrain but assures that it can be controlled with constant endeavour and dispassion. In brief, it is the secret of human civilization and culture that any objective howsoever lofty it may be, can be achieved through focusing the mind and making determined endeavour.

Human history bears testimony to the remarkable achievements of the focused and disciplined mind – from the discovery of fire and the invention of the wheel to the development of spaceship and Artificial intelligence. Every major step in human progress is the result of determined, concentrated and disciplined thinking.

Thus, while the mind's raw energy can be violent and destructive, it can also be a great creative force when controlled and directed wisely. The practice of yoga, as expounded in the Gita, offers a roadmap to harness the mind's power and usher in an era of peace, prosperity, and happiness, both at individual and collective levels.

Ultimately, the direction of our intellect, the use of our resources, and the focus of our mind will determine the quality of our lives and the future of humanity.

Key Learnings

- The basic nature of the mind is to waver and rush through innumerable thoughts. A focused mind is essential to tackle complex problems.
- The greatest challenge in life is to master the mind and remain composed amid the chaotic rush of issues and options.

- One who has learnt to control his mind and is at peace with himself is unaffected by the dualities of existence.
- A leader must be alert and aware of his own thoughts, act with wisdom and discernment, and stay cool and calm while making major decision.
- The only way to control the mind is through rigorous practice (abhyasa) and developing an attitude of detachment (vairagya).

•••••

Success Mantra 10

Be Even-Minded

A leader must not only be skilled in managing day-to-day affairs of an organization but also excel in crafting long-term strategies that ensure sustained success. A leader, regardless of the nature of his organisation, is always exposed to various forces that watch and evaluate his performance on a regular basis. In the corporate world, he has to gauge the market, evaluate the competition, maintain an edge over other competitors, and achieve set targets. It requires visionary leadership to plan, arrange resources, monitor deployment and progress, develop the brand image and reach its target groups.

A leader needs to be fully aware of the current circumstances in which he operates and be capable enough to accurately predict what may happen tomorrow and further into the future as well. He has to be alert and, in a position to respond to any emergent exigency in the environment.

A leader has to tackle all sorts of situations with maturity and balance. He should not be carried away with success and also never permit himself to be perturbed by setbacks and failures.

R.W. Emerson has very aptly said, 'The hero is a mind of such balance that no disturbances can shake his will, but pleasantly, and, as it were, merrily, he advances to his own music, alike in frightful alarms and in the tipsy mirth of universal dissoluteness.'

The primary requisite for a leader is to know his organisation from within and keep himself updated about the forces and factors affecting it. The wisdom enshrined in the Gita has eternal relevance to act as a guide for all situations. During India's struggle for independence, all freedom fighters, right from Bal Gangadhar Tilak to Chandra Shekhar Azad and Subhash Chandra Bose, derived their inspiration from the Gita. Mahatma Gandhi, the great apostle of non-violence, took refuge in this text whenever his mind was agitated. It speaks volumes about the inclusiveness and relevance of the Gita.

In the human mind there are incessant conflicts between opposing forces—of good and bad, right and wrong. A competent leader is always sensitive to the stakes and context while responding to a situation. The Gita provides a clear roadmap to help one choose judiciously even in the most trying situations. One of the major challenges leaders face is to correctly assess both the prevailing situation and the future needs, as related to the values, beliefs and requirements of their ecosystem. Often, leaders are faced with situations where conflicting emotions and values pose equally difficult options and choices. In such cases, the Gita is the best guide—and has been so through generations.

Leaders have to be cool, competent and visionary while formulating policies for the betterment of their organisations.

Innovative policies and decisions make a leader stand out and lead his organisation to great heights. The art of handling tough situations in a balanced manner requires competence, deftness as well as maturity. Leaders need to be decisive in conflicting situations and use discretion in the light of their own perception and wisdom.

The Gita repeatedly emphasises the importance of balanced mindset and detachment:

योगस्थः कुरु कर्माणि संगं त्यक्त्वा धनंजय ।
सिद्ध्यसिद्ध्योःसमो भूत्वा समत्वं योग उच्यते।।

(अध्याय 2/48)

Yogasthah kurukarmani sangam tyaktvaa Dhananjaya.
Siddhyasiddhyoh samo bhutvaa samatvam yoga uchyate.

(Chapter 2/48)

(*O Arjuna! Perform your duties with equanimity, abandoning attachment; being even-minded in success and failure is called yoga.*)

The central theme of the Gita is to act without attachment, treating success and failure alike. A leader must perform their duties with perfect composure, remaining indifferent to the results. Acts performed with an even mind abandoning attachment and treating success and failure alike is called yoga. A leader must act with perfect calmness, remain impartial and just, and develop an integrated personality where thoughts, words and actions align with the greater goal of the organization. A competent leader should not only be able to control the agitations of his mind but also transcend his own whims and fancies.

The Gita lays great emphasis on the importance of actions performed dispassionately advising leaders to face success and failure with equanimity. This state of equilibrium is essential for a leader to remain composed in the face of life's challenges. Maintaining a balanced view is of great help to a leader as being cool and have an even temperament imparts great strengths and foresight to a leader.

Krishna describes the qualities of a person with unwavering composure in the following shloka:

यः सर्वत्रानभिस्नेहस्तत्तत्प्राप्य शुभाशुभम् ।
नाभिनन्दति न द्वेष्टि तस्य प्रज्ञा प्रतिष्ठिता ।।

(अध्याय 2/57)

Yah sarvatraanabhisnehastat-tat praapya shubhaashubham
Naabhinandati na dveshti tasya prajnaa pratisthitaa.

(Chapter 2/57)

(*One who is unattached in all circumstances, who does not rejoice or despises upon receiving good or evil, their intellect is firmly established.*)

A leader should be a person of even composure and be able to view the happenings of life with maturity and vision. For a long and meaningful journey, one must take the twists and turns of life in his stride, and be unaffected by the vagaries of outcomes.

It is essential for a successful leader to use one's discretion and not get carried away by extraneous opinions and views. One has to be in full control of oneself and never be guided by instinct or ego. One should not act on instincts or ego as it is fraught with risks and failure:

Krishna further explains that lack of control over the senses leads to deviation from one's path:

इन्द्रियाणां हि चरतां यन्मनोऽनुविधीयते।
तदस्य हरति प्रज्ञां वायुर्नावमिवाम्भसि।।

(अध्याय 2/67)

Indriyaanaam hi charataam yanmano nuvidheeyate
Tadasya harati prajnaam vaayurnaavamivaambhasi

(Chapter 2/67)

(Just as the wind sweeps a boat off its course, even one of the senses on which the mind focuses can lead the intellect astray.)

This shloka emphasises the importance of an even attitude and the necessity of retaining complete control on the senses. The example of a boat sailing in the water being forcefully carried away off its course by strong winds is very relevant, because in absence of self-control, the relentless pursuit of even one of the senses is enough to cause a deviation from one's chartered road map. This ultimately leads to chaos and anarchy in one's life as well as in an organisation.

Competing desires create agitation in the human mind and influence the decision-making abilities of a person. This is because a mind under the strong influence of urges, passions, attachments or aversions loses its direction. Once it becomes the pattern of behaviour, a person loses his power of discretion and with it, his control over his senses. It is a dangerous situation for anybody, more so for a leader who has to act on behalf of his organisation and whose actions affect the interest and destiny of a large number of people.

Krishna explains to Arjuna the importance of retaining strong control on one's senses:

तस्माद्यस्य महाबाहो निगृहीतानि सर्वशः।
इन्द्रियाणीन्द्रियार्थेभ्यस्तस्य प्रज्ञा प्रतिष्ठिता।।

(अध्याय 2/68)

Tasmaadyasya mahaabaaho nigriheetaani sarvashah
Indriyaaneendriyaarthebhayastasya prajnaa pratisthitaa.

(Chapter 2/68)

(*Therefore, one whose senses are completely restrained from their objects, O mighty armed, he is firmly established in intellect.*)

We should be fully conscious of the adverse consequences of actions based on instinct and the allure of sensory objects. For success in life, one should be wise enough to avoid the urges of the senses and act with discretion. Aversion is equally to be avoided as attachments and aversion both blur the intellect and render a person incapable of using his discretion and choosing the right course.

The eternal wisdom of the Gita provides a distinct roadmap, not only for leading a meaningful life, but also for developing sterling leadership qualities. A leader can handle any situation and surmount any difficulty if he maintains his composure and uses his intellect with discretion. Following the precepts of the Gita, one can lead a life full of meaning and substance and successfully face any hurdle in life.

Therefore, for a person whether he is a householder or a leader of an organisation, the wisdom contained in the Gita is the ultimate guide to lead a life of success and dignity. The text provides a time-tested and time-trusted roadmap for the journey of life through whatever terrain and climate it is destined to pass.

Key Learnings

- A mind dominated by urges, passions, attachments or aversions loses its direction, and the ability to exercise discretion.

- The relentless pursuit of even one of the senses is enough to cause a deviation from one's chartered road map.
- A leader should be a person of even composure and be able to view the happenings of life with maturity and vision.
- One must take the twists and turns of life in his stride and remain unaffected by the vagaries of outcomes for a long and meaningful journey of life.
- Acts performed with a balanced mind, treating success and failure alike is called yoga.

•••••

Success Mantra **11**

Fire is Never Quenched by Adding Fuel

It is often said that the greatest victory is the one when a person conquers himself. Those who cannot command their own impulses and desires can never truly command others.

As Lao Tzu wisely putted, "*Mastering others is strength. Mastering yourself is true power.*"

It is important to understand that acts done under the influence of desire, anger or jealousy invariably weaken the position of a person and limit his abilities and options. In the course of time, such acts accumulate and become a burden, not only for oneself but also for his family or the organisation one happens to lead.

To become a success, one should learn to command himself, control his desires and curb the urges to act without discretion. Discretion is the wisdom to understand the difference between right and wrong, and also the propriety of response in a given context. All great men in history have been great masters of self-control who used discretion in all their acts and deeds.

Nelson Mandela suffered tremendously during his struggle for freedom, but when he became the president of South Africa with all the authority under his command, he demonstrated incredible self-control and exemplary discretion in his decisions and activities.

People act according to their basic nature and leanings and follow their natural propensities. However, if a person cannot exercise self-control, external restraints have little effect on their conduct. At the same time, it is not possible for anybody to suddenly transform his nature and renounce his natural leanings.

Krishna cautions Arjuna about human nature and the importance of exercising control:

इन्द्रियस्येन्द्रियस्यार्थे रागेद्वेषौ व्यवस्थितौ।
तयोर्न वशमागच्छेत्तौ ह्यस्य परिपन्थिनौ।।

(अध्याय 3/34)

Indriyasyendriyasyaarthe raagadveshau vyavasthitau
Tayorna vashamaagachchhettau hyasya paripanthinau.

(Chapter 3/34)

(*The attachment and aversion are situated in the objects of the senses. Let no one come under their sway, for they are the obstacles in the path.*)

The moment mind comes in contact with the sense objects, it is influenced by attachment or aversion which is situated in the objects. Therefore, we have to use our discretion with intellect and not become victims of our urges and impulses. If we fall prey to them, our life becomes directionless and devoid of wisdom. In such situations attachments and aversions take over and determine our thoughts and actions.

Acts based solely on our attachments and aversions create a chain of actions and reactions that eventually lead to great misery and suffering. It creates its own traps and bondages. When we do not listen to the craving of the senses—and the attachments and aversions dictated by our mind—we are in full control of ourselves and can avoid the trap. When we reach a state where pleasure and pain do not affect us, we experience true freedom and life acquires entirely a new dimension.

A leader must be extremely cautious about their thoughts and actions, and never act under the influence of sense cravings. The ability to control impulses and act with discretion is a fundamental attribute of any successful leader.

Arjuna, seeking to understand the root cause of human behaviour, asks Krishna to clarify why a person, even against their will, is sometimes compelled to commit sinful acts:

अथ केन प्रयुक्तोऽयं पापं चरति पुरूषः।
अनिच्छन्नपि वार्ष्णेय बलादिव नियोजितः।।

(अध्याय 3/36)

Atha kena prayuktoyam paapam charati poorushah
Anichchhannapi Vaarshneya balaadiva niyojitah.

(Chapter 3/36)

(*Then, by whom is a person impelled to commit sin, even against their will, O Vaarshneya?*)

Decisions taken without due thought and prudence create complications. Arjuna wants to know the reasons and motives behind such decisions that a man feels compelled to take even against his will. His curiosity is genuine, because often, a person commits sinful acts that he has never meditated upon and which appear alien even to their basic instincts.

It is observed that many acts of a dubious nature are committed by people who are well educated, mature and possess sound reasoning. Arjuna has a very pertinent query where he wants to know the underlying forces that make a person do wrongful acts.

As a true mentor, Krishna explains the root cause for such acts:

काम एष क्रोध एष रजोगुणसमुद्भवः।
महाशनो महापाप्मा विद्ध्येनमिह वैरिणम्।।

(अध्याय 3/37)

Kaama esha krodha esha rajogunasamudbhavah
Mahaashano Mahaapaapmaa viddhyenamiha vairinam

(Chapter 3/37)

(*It is desire and anger, born of the mode of passion which is all-devouring and most sinful. Know this to be the enemy here.*)

According to the Gita, it is desire arising out of passion which leads to anger and creates a cycle of thoughts and actions which cause misery and suffering in life. This cycle goes on perpetuating the cause-and-effect sequence and keeps a person trapped in its whirlpool. Once self-control is lost and a person begins acting on impulses, the descent has no end, for it is all-devouring and all-polluting.

It is said that desire, by its sheer scale and intensity, overpowers a person's psyche and makes him incapable of discriminating between right and wrong.

Often, people accept it as part of human nature, but impulses such as desire, anger, jealousy, hatred, violence, etc., are manifestations of baser urges and must be nipped in the bud. These impulses are not an integral part of human nature and one should consider them to be one's greatest enemy. Although the pursuit of impulses induces a feeling of pleasure and pride, it ultimately proves to be the root cause of all affliction and suffering.

Passion leads to attachment, which gives rise to anger. Anger in turn causes delusion and loss of discretion, which eventually results in great agony and suffering. If a person is able to exercise self-control and use his discretion, they will be able to eliminate all negative emotions like lust, anger and aversion.

The previous shloka also emphasises that impulses are insatiable and if not controlled, keep emerging in a variety of different forms. Passion has been rightly described in the shloka as being grossly wicked. The adjective used for lust and anger born of passion in the shloka is *mahaapaapmaa*, which literally means great sinner. It is passion alone that leads one to attachment towards sensory objects and drags him to sinful acts and deeds.

Krishna further emphasises the overwhelming power of desire:

आवृतं ज्ञानमेतेन ज्ञानिनो नित्यवैरिणा।
कामरूपेण कौन्तेय दुष्पूरेणानलेन च।।

(अध्याय 3/39)

Aavritam jnaanametena jnaanino nityavairinaa
Kaamarupena Kaunteya dushpoorenaanalena cha.

(Chapter 3/39)

(O son of Kunti, knowledge is enveloped by this eternal enemy of the wise in the form of desire, which is insatiable, like fire.)

Desire is never satiated even when it is fulfilled, much like how fire cannot be quenched by adding fuel to it. Desire is the eternal enemy, even of those who are endowed with knowledge and discretion. Desire, in fact, is the real enemy, as it drags everybody on to the path of undesirable activities which ultimately lead to doom and destruction. The greatest irony is that people enamoured by the senses indulge in sense gratification and consider it to be the mark of success and achievement. This is what the Gita cautions against. The devil of desire drives people to acts that are against their better judgement and lands them in trouble.

Therefore, one of the key attributes of a leader is the ability to exercise self-control and restraint desires. By doing so, a leader is able to view situations in their proper context and perspective. A leader, who is disciplined and exercises discretion is in a much better position to face any eventuality. Such a leader can handle any situation with competence and lead their team to success.

Key Learnings

- Desire, born of passion, leads to lust and anger and a cycle of negative thoughts and actions, which causes agony and suffering.
- Actions driven by lust, anger and jealousy weaken the position of a leader and limit their ability to lead effectively.
- Discretion is the wisdom to be conscious and cautious about the values of one's decisions and deeds.

- Desire, like fire, can never be satiated, no matter how much it is fed.
- A leader who can exercise self-control and discretion will be able to eliminate negative emotions such as lust, anger and aversion, leading their organisation to greater success.

•••••

Success Mantra **12**

Nothing as Purifying as Knowledge

Leadership is not confined to a specific situation or a particular position; it is a state of being. A true leader prepare himself to face life's challenges with vision, responsibility and resolve, undeterred by obstacles.

Leadership is an evolving process, where one endeavours to achieve set objectives using available resources while willingly accepting responsibility for leading the organisation. The main purpose of the Gita is to awaken Arjuna the warrior to realise his true self and understand the nature of duty in the given context. A true leader has to be much more than just the head of an entity; he has to be a person willing to take risks, do his best to further the interest of his organisation and take responsibility for its success and failure.

Jack Welch once said, 'Before you are a leader, success is all about growing yourself. When you become a leader, success is all about growing others.' This is the ideal that true leaders embrace and strive toward.

It is often said that a leader is someone who knows the way, goes the way, and shows the way. However, the true key to successful leadership is not the exercise of power and authority, but rather the ability to exert influence.

The main responsibility of a leader is to evolve a vision, translate it into reality by utilising the resources in the best possible manner and leading the group to achieve its aims and objectives. Leadership is a journey, not towards power and prestige, but towards actualising the dreams, ambitions, plans and programmes of the organisation the leader happens to lead.

True leadership is a long-drawn process and requires keen learning and constant endeavour to ensure success and well-being of the people involved. Learning requires genuine interest and rigorous pursuit without being obsessed with the position, as well as the wisdom to use discretion. For a great leader, knowledge and the keenness to learn are of paramount importance. A leader needs to have clear understanding of objectives, problems and resources available before he charts out the roadmap to achieve a target.

The Gita underscores the importance of knowledge in the following shloka:

न हि ज्ञानेन सदृशं पवित्रमिह विद्यते।
तत्स्वयं योगसंसिद्धः कालेनात्मनि विन्दति।।

(अध्याय 4 / 38)

Na hi jnaanena sadrisham pavitramiha vidyate.
Tatsvayam yogasamsiddhah kaalenaatmani vindati.

(Chapter 4/38)

(*There is nothing in this world as purifying as knowledge. One who is established in yoga perceives this in his self over time.*)

The Gita states unequivocally that there is nothing as purifying as knowledge in this world. The continuous practice of yoga elevates a human being and enables him to understand life's truth and see the world in the right perspective. Knowledge is all-purifying; it removes ignorance and darkness, liberates a person from various bondages and elevates him to an exalted position. It is knowledge which enables a person to distinguish between light and darkness, and right and wrong. All kinds of misery and suffering arise due to lack of knowledge. Arjuna's delusion just before the war is about to start is a glaring example of the lack of knowledge to understand the truth of the situation and make up one's mind to do one's duty in the given context.

It is through knowledge that we understand life and realise the truth, which enables us to take appropriate decisions in complex situations. The practice of yoga in the context of leadership implies the condition where a leader is able to transcend the feelings of attachment to actions as well as the fruits of action. In such a situation, the actions of a leader are carried out with careful consideration, balance and discretion. According to the Gita, these are the traits of a true leader—a leader of substance and integrity.

The Gita is the best scripture to impart right knowledge to enable us to live a divine life and fulfil our duties. Krishna advises Arjuna on how to approach a learned person in order to gain this knowledge:

तद्विद्धि प्रणिपातेन परिप्रश्नेन सेवया।
उपदेक्ष्यन्ति ते ज्ञानं ज्ञानिनस्तत्त्वदर्शिनः।।

(अध्याय 4/34)

Tadviddhi pranipaatena pariprashnena sevayaa
Upadekshyanti te jnaanam jnaaninastattvadarshinah.

(Chapter 4/34)

(*Learn the truth by prostrating, questioning and serving. Men of knowledge who have realised the truth will instruct you that knowledge.*)

Krishna tells Arjuna to approach learned teachers with reverence and learn through enquiry and service. This is true even today. Those who are well-versed and have experience can provide true guidance to a genuine and humble learner. To travel far in life, it is essential to be humble and to be keen to acquire knowledge from all possible sources.

According to the Gita, faith, reverence and sincerity are of prime importance for learning from a guru. A learner must approach their mentor with humility, trust and genuine respect, as well as be willing to render service to earn the guru's confidence and grace.

The Gita describes the attributes of a genuine learner and the benefits of knowledge:

श्रद्धावान् लभते ज्ञानं तत्परः संयतेन्द्रियः।
ज्ञानं लब्ध्वा परां शान्तिमचिरेणाधिगच्छति।।

(अध्याय 4/39)

Shraddhaavaan labhate jnaanam tatparah samyatendriyah.
Jnaanam labdhvaa paraam shantimchirenaadhigachhati.

(Chapter 4/39)

(*One having deep faith and control on their senses, and is devoted to their efforts attains knowledge. Having gained knowledge, they quickly attains supreme peace.*)

This shloka describes faith, self-control and devotion as three basic prerequisites for attaining knowledge. It further says that after gaining knowledge, one quickly attains supreme peace.

One who lacks faith can never learn, no matter how great the teacher may be or how relentless the efforts. The art of learning largely depends on the degree of faith in the guru, perseverance and willingness to sacrifice ease, pleasure and comfort. Faith, self-control and determined effort are the attributes required for knowledge and success in life.

Faith is one of the most important ingredients to achieve success and acclaim. Faith in one's beliefs, capabilities and methods, faith in one's team and faith in one's aims and objectives are needed for a leader to lead an organisation to success and positive, long-term consequences. To have the unflinching faith of his colleagues and followers is the first requirement for any leader to achieve significant results. Mahatma Gandhi, Nelson Mandela, Abraham Lincoln and Mother Teresa all enjoyed unstinted faith and support of not only their colleagues and followers, but also people at large, even those who did not agree with their views or methods.

Key Learnings

- Leadership is not confined to a specific situation or position; it requires vision, responsibility and resolve, undeterred by challenges.
- A true leader is much more than the head of an organization; they must be willing to take risks, do their best for the organisation's benefit, and take responsibility for its outcomes.
- The primary duty of a leader is to create a vision, translate it into reality, and use available resources efficiently to achieve their goals.

- Leadership is not about power and position but rather a responsibility for leading an organization towards fulfilling its aims and objectives.
- All great leaders enjoyed unstinted faith and support of not only their followers but also people at large, even those who disagreed with them.

•••••

Success Mantra **13**

Selfish Motives Limit Initiatives

The foremost responsibility of a leader is to create an environment in which the members of the team are able to attain peak performance in their allocated sectors. A great leader is not judged merely by their own achievements, but by their ability to inspire, guide, and enable their team to achieve collective goals. True leadership lies in the skill of uplifting and empowering others to accomplish organizational tasks.

A true leader must strive to be just and fair in discharge of duties. He should never develop cliques or favourites. He should enable all people working for the organisation with the same intent and support to do their best. This enhances the acceptability of a leader and keeps the team united. At the same time, a leader should not assume that whatever success is achieved is only because of his merit and leadership. The credit of success should also go to the members of his team, and they should be evaluated strictly according to their merit and contribution.

Krishna emphasises this aspect of leadership in the following shloka:

विद्याविनयसम्पन्ने ब्राह्मणे गवि हस्तिनि।
शुनि चैव श्वपाके च पण्डिताः समदर्शिनः।।

(अध्याय 5/18)

Vidyaavinayasampanne braahmane gavi hastini
Shuni chaiva shvapaake cha panditaah samadarshinah.

(Chapter 5/18)

(*The truly wise view a learned and cultured Brahmin, a cow, an elephant, a dog and an outcast with an equal eye.*)

Krishna tells Arjuna that the prime quality of a leader is to eliminate distinction in his dealings, even in cases where distinction is a norm for common people.

The ability to exercise equality of vision needs rigorous training and self-control of one's thoughts and actions. It requires reorientation of the mindset and constant self-observation. Equality of vision emanates from the realisation of unity of spirit across all divisions of birth, caste, creed, space and time. Throughout the Gita, Krishna tries to make Arjuna widen his vision regarding relationships and situations and evaluate the circumstance and role of people in a just and proper context.

A true leader must not be obsessed with the feeling of being the key doer and should not be given to pretensions. He should be competent enough to take control of his ego and not entertain doership notions. A successful leader knows that in performing various tasks and achieving organisational goals, multiple forces act in tandem and the role of everybody involved is valuable.

This point has been clearly explained by Krishna in the following shloka:

नैव किन्चत्करोमीति युक्तो मन्येत तत्त्ववित्।
पश्यन्श्रृण्वन्स्पृशन्जिघ्रन्नश्नन्गच्छन्स्वपन्श्वसन्।
प्रलपन्विसृजन्गृहन्नुन्मिषन्निमिषन्नपि।
इन्द्रियाणीन्द्रियार्थेषु वर्तन्त इति धारयन्।।

(अध्याय 5/8–9)

Naiva kinchit karomiti yukto manyeta tattvavit
Pashyan srinvansprishan jighrannashnan gachchan svapanshvasan
Pralapanvisrijangrihnannunmishannimishannapi
Indriyaanindriyaartheshu vartanta iti dhaarayan.

(Chapter 5/8-9)

(*The one who knows the truth, thinks 'I do nothing at all'; in seeing, hearing, touching, smelling, tasting, walking, sleeping, breathing, speaking, emitting, grasping, and opening and closing the eyes, they hold that it is only senses acting upon their respective objects.*)

It is natural human tendency to take pride in their actions whenever they perform anything significant. This notion is not right, and in reality, it's a great barrier in elevating one's consciousness beyond the sense of 'doership'. But for a person who is well-established in yoga, such a barrier has no meaning. Because with his divine knowledge and elevated consciousness, he sees his 'self' as separate from the material body, and truly understands that all activities are the result of the senses indulging with their objects.

The preceding shlokas describe the process of internalising the notion that any kind of human activity happens in accordance with the laws of nature. The main wisdom emphasised in the shlokas is to understand that entertaining the perception of one's own 'doership' is neither right nor does it serve any worthwhile purpose. This realisation enables a leader to remain calm and composed, because he who is not obsessed with the sense of 'doership' will find it easier to exercise equanimity in all his thoughts and deeds. This realisation is very crucial for a leader who wishes to travel far, as ups and downs in the course of performing the duties of a leader are inevitable.

Therefore, for a leader, the realisation that success is achieved by the involvement and contribution of all stakeholders has many positive implications. It saves a leader from arrogance, enhances his acceptability and helps him in remaining cool, calm and collected in case of setbacks and failures. Leaders who are prone to egocentric behaviour very soon lose ground and invariably meet their doom. It is observed that quite often, the downfall of a leader is caused not because of any lack of merit on his part, but as a consequence of his egocentric and erratic behaviour.

A true leader is aware that leadership is an opportunity to serve a cause and it is their dharma to perform their duties with full devotion, without becoming overly attached to the position or to the outcomes.

Such a leader perceives their role as part of a larger divine order, and understands that actions are an interplay of nature's forces, not merely their personal achievement.

Krishna further clarifies this philosophy of action in the following shloka:

कायेन मनसा बुद्ध्या केवलैरिन्द्रियैरपि।
योगिनः कर्म कुर्वन्ति संगम त्यक्त्वात्मशुद्धये।।

(अध्याय 5/11)

Kaayena manasaa buddhyaa kevalairindriyairapi Yoginah karma kurvanti sangam tyaktvaatmashuddhaye.

(Chapter 5/11)

(Yogis, giving up attachment, perform actions with body, mind and intellect, or even the senses alone, solely for self-purification.)

Krishna explains to Arjuna that true leaders try neither to meet their own selfish ends nor do they entertain any feelings of self-importance. They perform all their actions in detached spirit having no sense of doership. This awareness is of supreme importance and should be internalised by leaders, whatever their context or situation. The shloka further emphasises that the only purpose behind the endeavours of a truc leader is to serve the organisation and, in the process, elevate oneself. Krishna calls it self-purification— the purification of mind and intellect, which is said to be the greatest purpose of human life.

In response to Arjuna's curiosity about the self-purification and its significance, Krishna says:

युक्तः कर्मफलं त्यक्त्वा शान्तिमाप्नोति नैष्ठिकीम्
अयुक्तः कामकारेण फले सक्तो निबध्यते।।

(अध्याय 5/12)

Yuktah karmaphalam tyaktvaa shaantimaapnoti naishthikeem
Ayuktah kaamakaarena phale sakto nibadhyate

(Chapter 5/12)

(Having given up the fruit of action, a yogi attains lasting peace; while the one, who is impelled by their desire get tied down with fruits of their actions.)

Krishna clarifies that detachment from any kind of desire is the route to achieving peace, but those others who remain entangled in worldly desires, perform every action with a sense of attachment and anticipation of their fruits. The attachment with actions and the results binds a doer in many ways and leads to the loss of freedom, creating anxiety and limitation. This shloka offers great wisdom for leaders, as it very clearly defines the sterling qualities of an effective leader—not to be attached to actions and its fruits and never seek to further self-interest. These create limitations to his personal growth and inhibit the freedom of a leader in taking decisions, and motivating his team to perform in the sole interest of the organisation.

Key Learnings

- A great leader is known not by their personal achievements but by their ability in inspiring and motivating their team to achieve common goals.
- A leader should not assume that whatever success is achieved is only because of him.
- It is observed that quite often, the downfall of a leader is caused not from lack of competence, but from their egocentric and erratic behaviour.
- A true leader is aware that leadership is an opportunity to serve a cause, and it is their dharma to do their duties with full devotion.
- The sole purpose behind every action of a true leader is to serve the organisation and, in the process, elevate oneself.

•••••

Success Mantra **14**

Transcending Rewards

Many of us go through life as if it is someone else's responsibility to give meaning to our existence. Yet the truth remains that our livesare as meaningful and wonderful as we choose and strive to make them. In any social environment, we lead our lives in consciousness of cooperation and concern for one another. Nobody lives in a vacuum and it's a great torture to live in isolation. The quality of day-to-day life depends upon our philosophy, vision, co-operation and concern we have for others, and the responses we get from them. These again depend on the traditions, values, aspirations and the culture of the people we live, interact and work with. The quality of our life depends on what kind of person we are, and the kinds of persons we socialise and interact with.

In the following shloka, Krishna tells Arjuna that there are four kinds of people who seek God:

चतुर्विधा भजन्ते मां जनाः सुकृतिनोऽर्जुन।
आर्तो जिज्ञासुरर्थार्थी ज्ञानी च भरतर्षभ।।

(अध्याय 7/16)

Chaturvidha bhajante mam janah sukrtino'rjuna.
Arto jijnasurartharthijnanicha Bharatarshabha.

(Chapter 7/16)

(*O best of Bharatas! Four kinds of devotees of noble deeds worship Me: the distressed, the seeker of knowledge, the seeker of wealth and the man of wisdom.*)

Most people belong to the first three categories of devotees; it's the people belonging to the fourth who are especially distinguished as they have realised the truth of the 'self'. Such people understand the reality and have an enlightened view of life. They are true leaders who set an example and show the right path to their followers. They are able to lead people from darkness to light, from bondage to freedom, enhancing joy and happiness and reducing suffering in the world.

Most people desire wealth, prestige and power because they believe that these will bring happiness and security. However, the question remains whether material goods can really lead to happiness. In reality, such people never attain true happiness as material possessions rarely lead to happiness, rather they fuel a self-perpetuating cycle of lust, greed and anger, which further causes pain and suffering in life.

The central theme of the Gita is that the root cause of all grief and suffering is desire and desire never leads to real joy and meaning in life. We all need air, water, food and shelter for our basic survival. Once these needs are satisfied, they are quickly followed by the need for safety, security, love and a sense of belonging. Most people consider their lives to be happy and successful if these needs are fulfilled in accordance with their expectations.

It's a common observation that material things offer happiness only up to a point. Many individuals stop at this level and still feel happy and content with their life, whereas some people continue their onward and upward journey to the next level of realising their potential and doing something significant for the community, the society and the world. Such people belong to the fourth category mentioned in the shloka and are true leaders, irrespective of their context of time and space.

Krishna establishes the importance of such people by saying that they are most dear to Him:

तेषां ज्ञानी नित्ययुक्त एकभक्तिर्विशिष्यते।
प्रियो हि ज्ञानिनोऽत्यर्थमहं स च मम प्रियः।।

(अध्याय 7/17)

Tesham jnani nityayukta ekabhaktirvishishyate.
Priyo hi jnanino'tyarthamaham sa cha mam priyah.

(Chapter 7/17)

(*Among these, I consider wise persons to be the best who worship me with steadfast and exclusive devotion. I am dear to them and they are dear to Me.*)

Krishna, stressing on the importance of wisdom and single-mindedness, states that amongst the four types of worshippers, people belonging to the fourth category are the ones who are on the right track and moving in right direction. Krishna raises the pedestal of wise devotees who have internalised the knowledge that material things are transitory and the real purpose of human life is being in constant union with God. The position of a devotee who worships God with true knowledge and steadfast devotion is supreme among the devotees. Unwavering devotion makes a person pure-hearted and detached from the world. A stage comes during the evolution of such a person when his devotion becomes truly exclusive and steadfast.

A wise person who is in union with the divine and fully devoted is free from all attachments and cravings. Such a person is able to pursue the right objectives, choose the right paths, follow the right means, and find the right companions. Leaders like Mahatma Gandhi, Abraham Lincoln, Martin Luther King Jr, Nelson Mandela and Mother Teresa all belong to this category. These are the people who changed the world and showed the direction not only to the people they led in their own life times but also to future generations.

The Gita very clearly highlights the path of evolution for the man of wisdom. Krishna tries to make Arjuna understand the ultimate reality of human life and follow his dharma in the given situation. Krishna, through his discourses, tries to elevate Arjuna from the mundane level of attachment and fear to a higher level of consciousness. Only this could enlighten him about his prescribed duties as per his station in life.

It's very important for a leader to understand the matrix of his organisation, as well as the ecosystem he has to operate in. A leader should be able to clearly comprehend the situation and attempt a solution keeping all factors in view in a detached manner. Leadership requires the highest level of integrity and an attitude to approach every problem with vision and clarity. The quality of a leader depends on the values he cherishes and the standards he sets for himself. What is most important for a leader is to convey his message not so much through words as by his attitude and actions. Leadership is nothing but the ability to impact, influence and inspire their team.

It is important for a leader to self-actualise before he makes any effort to get ahead of other people. This can be termed as self-awareness or self-realisation. Krishna emphasises this point in the following shloka:

वेदेषु यज्ञेषु तपःसु चैव
दानेषु यत्पुण्यफलं प्रदिष्टम्।
अत्येति तत्सर्वमिदं विदित्वा
योगी परं स्थानमुपैति चाद्यम्।।

(अध्याय 8/28)

Vedeshu yajneshu tapahsu chaiva
daaneshu yatpunyaphalam pradishtam
Atyeti tatsarvamidam viditvaa
Yogi param sthaanamupaiti chaadyam

(Chapter 8/28)

(*The yogi, having known all this, transcends the rewards of meritorious deeds assigned to the study of the Vedas, sacrifices, austerities and charities, and attains the supreme and eternal state.*)

Krishna tells Arjuna that the yogi is never enamoured by the rewards ensuing from study of the Vedas, sacrifices austerities and charities, etc. He is fully convinced that these are to be passed over by one willing to attain the supreme state. A yogi, while performing his worldly actions, keeps his mind focused on the ultimate objective of human life, unmindful of the actions as well as rewards resulting from his deeds, sacrifices and penances. Many people consider that study of scriptures, performance of sacrifices, observation of penance and giving charity etc., are actions of great spiritual significance, but according to the Gita, these acts are of minor consequence for a yogi. Unless we have true devotion to God, there is no deliverance from material bondage and suffering. A true yogi aims at freedom from worldly afflictions and perpetual bondage.

This example of a yogi is relevant for an enlightened leader, as such a person leaving aside the lure of authority, prestige and privileges endeavours to meet the ultimate objective of the organisation. This wisdom is of great significance for a true leader if he wishes to lead his team to spectacular results and serve society in an exemplary manner.

This shloka indicates an exalted ideal of leadership to which all leaders, whether leading a family, a corporate or a nation, should aspire. Only then can a leader lead his organisation to great heights and eminence.

Kery Learnings

- Our life is as meaningful and wonderful as we choose and strive to make it.
- People desire material gains as they believe that these can make them happy; however, material things offer happiness only up to a point.
- Leadership is nothing but the ability to impact, influence and inspire one's team.
- It is important for a leader to self-actualise before he makes any efforts to lead and guide others.
- The ideal of the yogi—detached, devoted, and focused is the timeless model of exemplary leadership.

•••••

Success Mantra **15**

The Essence of True Leadership

The real influence of a leader is not defined by his physical presence or the power exercised by him, but by the unity and coherence that persist in an organisation even when he is not around. The subtle authority of a leader unites various constituents of an organisation into one invisible entity. At such work places, people work towards achieving goals not because of the fear or the formal authority of the leader, but because of the feeling of solidarity they have with the organisation and its objectives. A leader who can create such solidarity is a true leader. Under his stewardship, even the sky is not the limit!

Krishna in the Gita, illustrates about the quality and influence of such a leader:

यथाकाशस्थितो नित्यं वायुः सर्वत्रगो महान्।
तथा सर्वाणि भूतानि मत्स्थानीत्युपधारय।।

(अध्याय 9/6)

Yathaakaashasthito nityam vaayuh sarvatrago mahaan
Tathaa sarvaani bhootaani matsthaaneetyupadhaaraya

(Chapter 9/6)

(*As the mighty wind moving everywhere, ever remains in space, know that in the same manner all existences abide in Me.*)

Krishna gives an analogy of air existing in space to enable Arjuna to understand the significance. The air cannot exist independent of the space. It may change its form, speed and other qualities, but it still remains within the space. In the same manner, everything existing in creation is never out of the sphere of divine influence. It simply exists due to divine will. Thus, all existence in the universe may be said to be abiding in God.

Extending this logic to the concept of leadership, it may be said that the subtle influence of a leader in an organisation should be pervasive and bind all to the source, although it may remain invisible. In the organisational context, this is the real test of the greatness of a leader. A leader should always strive to create such an influence. Real power should not require an open display. The great lesson to be learnt from the preceding shloka is that a true leader should act in such a way that the goals are internalised and actualised without ever feeling the force and pressure of authority.

A leader of significance does not require an overt display of his position and authority. Nelson Mandela, in his autobiography *Long Walk to Freedom*, says, "A leader is like a shepherd. He stays behind the flock, letting the most nimble go out ahead, whereupon the others follow, not realising that all along they are being directed from behind."

A leader should not be overbearing but should be capable of exercising his influence in a calm and quiet manner without being overtly authoritative. A leader should be free from egocentric thoughts and actions and be able to ensure desired results for the organisation. He should strive hard to conquer his ego and be in perfect control of the happenings in his organisation.

However, it is commonly accepted that it is easier said than done. To exercise such an influence, one has to control one's ego and act in a calm and quiet but determined manner.

Krishna offers a guiding principle to Arjuna on this path:

यत्करोषि यदश्नासि यज्जुहोषि ददासि यत्।
यत्तपस्यसि कौन्तेय तत्कुरुष्व मदर्पणम्।।

(अध्याय–9 / 27)

Yatkaroshi yadashnaasi yajjuhoshi dadaasi yat.
Yattapasyasi Kaunteya tatkurushva madarpanam.

(Chapter 9/27)

(*Whatever you do, whatever you eat, whatever you offer as oblation, whatever you gift, and whatever austerities you practise, O son of Kunti, do that as an offering to Me.*)

Krishna says that one should conduct all his activities with a conscious awareness of a supreme presence and higher purposes. We all know that for an organisation to succeed, everybody needs to do his best and achieve the goal. It is neither wise nor justified for a leader to take all the credit and bask in the glory of success. Krishna counsels Arjuna that by offering every act to Almighty God, one can avoid an overplay of ego and exercise control over one's thoughts and actions.

A leader should dedicate all his actions to the common good as a conscious contribution to the community and the society, without entertaining any sense of self-importance or self-glorification. Every moment and every action of a leader should be devoted to the act of serving his organisation keeping in view the primacy of higher purposes. In this way, a leader can abstain from egoism and exercise his influence in a calm, quiet and sustainable manner. All deeds and actions of such a leader become a source of inspiration and not only ensure great success but also enhance his prestige, influence and acceptability.

It is a matter of common observation that a person who wants to do everything himself and tries to garner all the credit can never perform great tasks. True leadership requires a great combination of character, grit and endeavour.

It is a fact that great leaders are known not as much by what they achieve but by their vision, effort and the influence of their persona and being. The lives of Abraham Lincoln, Mahatma Gandhi, Nelson Mandela and Mother Teresa speak eloquently about what they stood for and what they tried to achieve. Mahatma Gandhi summed up his philosophy of life with these words: 'My life is my message.'

In the course of life, people always strive hard to achieve some great position of authority and influence by using whatever means and methods possible, whereas a true leader is conscious of the appropriateness of the means being used and always focuses on strengthening his own self and enhancing his own intrinsic worth. The role of a leader is to ponder carefully and chart out a clear roadmap for his organisation. He should take into account intrinsic strengths, the external environment and, above all, the aims and objectives in terms of targets and goals that have been set to pursue growth.

Although one should bear in mind that in an organisational set-up, a leader is evaluated by his achievement in tangible terms and makes his reputation by being an achiever. In this process he is bound to identify himself with the achievement and take pride in them. However, the Gita abhors the feeling of attachment with actions, and also the concerns for the fruits of actions. According to the text, detachment from actions and its fruits gives a great sense of freedom and in the context of leadership, provides immense flexibility and space for a true leader to plan, execute and ensure great achievements. Detachment from actions and concerns for its results does not mean that one should be careless and unconcerned with the tenacity of effort or deployment of all the resources at hand. It only means that a leader acquires such a maturity and mastery over his emotions and attitudes that he is never bogged down by success or failure which ultimately affect his endeavours adversely in achieving his avowed objectives.

The secret of true leadership is not only in leading without explicit authority but also being able to inspire members of the team to be conscious of the ultimate objectives of the organisation and strive for assigned goals.

A leader must be impartial, accessible, and fair. This point is very clearly stated by Krishna in the following shloka:

समोऽहं सर्वभूतेषु न मे द्वेष्योऽस्ति न प्रियः।
ये भजन्ति तु मां भक्त्या मयि ते तेषु चाप्यहम्।।

(अध्याय 9/29)

Samoham sarvabhooteshu na me dveshyosti na priyah
Ye bhajanti tu maam bhaktyaa mayi te teshu chaapyaham.

(Chapter 9/29)

(*I am equally disposed to all beings; I favour none, nor do I hate anyone. But those who worship Me with devotion, they abide in Me and I, too, stand revealed to them.*)

This statement of Krishna to Arjuna stresses on the fact that a great leader should be accessible to all and should treat everybody equally, without any favour or malice. A leader should have no friends or foes in the organisation. He should be impartial and that should be evident through his thoughts, expressions and actions.

In essence, justice and fair play should be the core values in the dealings of a true leader, and they should walk their talk. His thoughts, words and actions should exhibit the same. Only then will people place their trust in him and will do their best to strengthen his hands and stand by him through thick and thin.

Key Learnings

- A true leader, without exercising power and authority, inspires people to internalise and achieve organizational goals.
- A leader should not be overbearing but should be capable of exercising his influence in a calm and quiet manner.
- A leader should dedicate all his actions to the greater good without entertaining any sense of self-glorification.

- A leader is known not as much by what he achieves but by the vision, effort and the influence of his own persona and the values he cherishes.

•••••

Success Mantra **16**

Pursuit of Excellence

It is said that great minds enjoy excellence, average minds love mediocrity and small minds adore comfort zones. Effective leaders bring people into new realms of excellence and motivate them to become distinguished in their respective fields.

Martin Luther King Jr has said, 'Everyone has the power for greatness, not for fame but for greatness.' Deep within our hearts, many of us feel that we are not living to our highest potential. Great leaders strive hard to do their best and be their best.

They are never satisfied with traditional wisdom, old practices and average performance. The test of leadership lies in taking the organisation beyond the status quo and exploring distant horizons and reaching greater heights. In fact, the pursuit of excellence is what defines the worth of a leader.

Leadership is an ever-evolving phenomenon. A true leader should always pursue expertise and enrichment in the form and content of his conduct towards his organisation. Pursuit of excellence is the desire to transcend known boundaries and travel on new paths to reach new destinations.

The Gita is a wonderful treatise; it inspires us to do our best and be our best. As the dialogue between Arjuna and Krishna progresses, Arjuna, being enamoured by His preaching, asks Krishna about the ways and forms of His manifestations:

कथं विद्यामहं योगिंस्त्वां सदा परिचिन्तयन्।
केषु केषु च भावेषु चिन्त्योऽसि भगवन्मया।।

(अध्याय 10/17)

Katham vidyaamaham yoginstvaam sadaa parichintayan
Keshu keshu cha bhaaveshu chintyosi Bhagavanmayaa.

(Chapter 10/17)

(*O Yogi, constantly meditating upon You, how may I know You? In what various forms should I think of You, O Blessed Lord?*)

Arjuna is keen to know the various dimensions of divine manifestations of Krishna that he should focus on while thinking about Him. In the previous shloka, Arjuna has two queries: firstly, he wants to know the ways by which he may practise constant remembrance, and secondly, he wants to understand the various manifestations so that he can fully comprehend the glory of Krishna.

In response, Krishna tells Arjuna that varied aspects of brilliance, power and excellence that one can see in existence are manifestations of His divine splendour. To make him further understand the glory, He mentions that a king amongst people, the Himalayas among immovable things and the lion among animals are illustrations of the above aspects of His glory. He further says that He is the victory of the victorious, goodness of the good, and spring—the season of flowers and fragrance—among the seasons.

Krishna further encapsulates his glory in a single powerful shloka:

यद्यद्विभूतिमत्सत्त्वं श्रीमदूर्जितमेव वा।
तत्तदेवावगच्छ त्वं मम तेजोंऽशसम्भवम्।।

(अध्याय 10/41)

Yadyadvibhutimatsattvam shrimadurjitameva vaa.
Tattadevaavagachha tvam mam tejomshasambhavam.

(Chapter 10/41)

(*Whatsoever is endowed with glory, brilliance and power, know that to be born from a spark of My splendour.*)

Krishna further elaborates by saying that every being that is brilliant, magnificent and mighty is a part manifestation of His glory. Although every aspect of creation is an expression of God's play, certain objects of nature that have great beauty and splendour are special manifestations of His magnificence. Similarly, every act of sacrifice, every work of great genius, every deed of heroism and every phenomenon of extraordinary beauty and brilliance is a revelation of His divine grace.

According to the Gita, God resides in the heart of every being, and every magnificent and powerful animate and inanimate object and creature existing in the universe is a manifestation of the divine glory. God is the infinite source of beauty, brilliance, power, knowledge and light. He is the ultimate source of life, energy and splendour from where all beings and material world derive their power, glory and sustenance.

In every act of dash, drive and success there are elements of divine grace and inspiration. The simple message for a leader from the shloka is that he should always pursue excellence, brilliance and acts of common goodness that provide strength, support and happiness to all.

Excellence is not an option; it is a calling. A true leader must constantly strive to reflect the divine spark through their thoughts, actions, and integrity.

Krishna concludes the narration to further enlighten Arjuna about His majesty:

नान्तोऽस्ति मम दिव्यानां विभूतीनां परन्तप।
एष तूद्देशतः प्रोक्तो विभूतेर्विस्तरो मया।।

(अध्याय 10/40)

Naantosti mama divyaanaam vibhooteenaam parantapa
Esha tooddeshatah prokto vibhootervistaro mayaa.

(Chapter 10/40)

(*There is no end to My divine manifestations, O Conqueror of foes. This is only a brief description given by Me about the extent of My glory.*)

These descriptions indicate that everybody should be conscious of beauty and splendour spread all around in existence, and derive inspiration to do his best in his sphere to add to it in whatever way he can. It is said that our success in life lies in leaving the world slightly better than the way we found it.

A true leader is aware of mighty forces working and shaping the world anew with each passing moment, and does his best to devise a new way, find a new path and choose a new destination for his family, organisation or country.

The great Chinese philosopher Confucius has said, "The will to win, the desire to succeed, the urge to reach your full potential... these are the keys that will unlock the door to personal excellence."

A great leader is always aware that excellence has no destination; it's a journey, a long and arduous one. It is a process of evolving, where a leader continuously strives to be his better self, a better motivator and a better leader. With this awareness, excellence no longer remains an act; it becomes a part of his life, a matter of belief and attitude.

Excellence is doing ordinary things in an extraordinary manner. As Winston Churchill wittily remarked:

"I am a man of simple tastes- I am easily satisfied with the best."

The message contained in the Gita in this context is that whatever one does should be done with full commitment, devotion and excellence.

The spirit of this message is echoed in this simple yet profound verse:

When I run, I run fast
When I read, time whirls past.
Whatever you do today,
Do it in the best possible way. – Cassondra

It is essential that a leader always remains in pursuit of excellence in all his thoughts and deeds. Excellence should be embedded deep in a leader's mind and awareness. Claude T. Bissell, a Canadian author has very aptly said:

"Excellence is the result of caring more than what others think is wise,

Risking more than what others consider safe,
Dreaming more than what others believe practical,
And expecting more than what others think is possible."

Key Learnings

- Great minds seek excellence, average minds accept mediocrity and small minds prefer comfort.
- The test of a true leader lies in their ability to challenge the status quo and reach new heights.
- The pursuit of excellence means transcending known boundaries and traveling on new paths with courage and conviction.
- Every act of sacrifice, every work of genius, every heroic deed and every phenomenon of extraordinary beauty and brilliance is a glimpse of divine grace.
- A true leader is always in pursuit of excellence in his thoughts, vision and actions.

•••••

Success Mantra **17**

Divine Destiny Ordains Everything

It is a matter of common understanding that the outcome of an individual's effort depends on their attitude towards work. Work provides not only material benefits and public recognition but also an opportunity for inner growth and satisfaction. If work is intellectually satisfying and emotionally fulfilling, it is not work; it's a piece of art and has tremendous potential for genuine happiness. A true leader gives his best to the task at hand and works with complete love and devotion.

The mystic poet Kahlil Gibran underlines the importance of working with love in the following lines:

> *You work that you may keep pace with the earth and the soul of the earth.*
>
> *For to be idle is to become a stranger unto the seasons, and to step out of life's procession, that marches in majesty and proud submission towards the infinite.*

Work is love made visible.

And if you cannot work with love but only with distaste, it is better that you should leave your work and sit at the gate of the temple and take alms of those who work with joy.

A true leader dedicates their intellect and life to the service of others. That is possible only when a person is able to transcend the limitation of his own concerns and devote his life to the cause of others by thinking of others, acting for others and living for others. Mahatma Gandhi elaborates this point in his autobiography:

"The best way to find your self is to lose yourself in the service of others."

Krishna inspires Arjuna to rise above the feelings of attachment and expectations, and perform his prescribed duties. In the following shloka, he asks him to be only an instrument in the events that are unfolding before him:

तस्मात्त्वमुत्तिष्ठ यशो लभस्व
जित्वा शत्रून्भुङ्क्ष्व राज्यं समृद्धम्।
मयैवैते निहताः पूर्वमेव
निमित्तमात्रं भव सव्यसाचिन्।।

(अध्याय 11/33)

Tasmaattvamuttishtha yasho labhasva
jitvaa Shatrunbhunkshva rajyam samriddham.
Mayaivaite nihataah purvameva
nimittamaatram bhava Savyasaachin.

(Chapter 11/33)

(Therefore, arise and win glory; conquer foes, enjoy the prosperous kingdom. These warriors have already been slain by Me, O Arjuna! Be only an instrument.)

Krishna tells Arjuna that divine destiny ordains that everything in the universe, including human beings, is only an instrument in a much larger game plan. Krishna assures Arjuna that his foes, standing arrayed in front of him on the battlefield, are as good as slain by the divine scheme of things and he has to only be an instrument.

In this divine game plan, the divine will is acted upon through human beings. Krishna's motive is to make Arjuna understand that he should not consider himself to be the principal doer; it is a divine design in which he has only to play his part in order to serve the larger purpose.

Some interpretations suggest that the meaning of the word 'foes' here indicates the feelings of attachment, ego, delusion and the sense of 'doership'. Krishna asks Arjuna to conquer these enemies, attain honour and enjoy the fruits of an accomplished life.

For a leader, the relevant message of this shloka is that one should work without any false ego of being a great doer, for in the scheme of divine design, a leader happens to be present there for the specific role. He should consider himself to be only an instrument in the process and merge his identity with the bigger purpose. The consequences of the actions follow their own course and should be accepted with equanimity.

A true leader should act to the best of his ability and competence, and shun any display of ego and pride. A leader who serves the organisation without any attachment and expectation is able to touch the inner chord in the consciousness of the people he intends to serve. Such a leader acquires the status of a true leader, a great leader—a leader of substance and consequence. Such a leader, by his actions and conduct, not only serves his organisation well but also leaves behind a legacy. They help to usher in a new age and new era, and change the direction of the thoughts and actions of their community, society and even the world.

History offers us numerous examples across the ages and the world. After the lives of Lord Ram, Lord Krishna, Jesus Christ, Buddha, Mahavira, Mahatma Gandhi, Abraham Lincoln, and Nelson Mandela, the world was never the same. Their leadership helped reshape the direction of thought and action, opening new eras and new paths for the humanity.

Another message of Krishna in this shloka is that the victory of the righteous people acting according to dharma, and the annihilation of the non-righteous ones acting against the tenets of dharma is the essence of divine design. Such a design that is aimed at establishing the supremacy of truth and justice ultimately wins the day whatever the odds or difficulties. In a way, it's a great opportunity and an act of divine blessing if a leader is chosen by the destiny to become an instrument of the divine design.

Krishna further emphasises the quality of such a true leader:

अनपेक्षः शुचिर्दक्ष उदासीनो गतव्यथः
सर्वारम्भपरित्यागी यो मदभक्तः स मे प्रियः।

(अध्याय 12/16)

Anapekshah shuchirdaksha udaaseeno gatavyathah
Sarvaarambhaparityaagee yo madbhaktah sa me priyah.

(Chapter 12/16)

(*Who expects nothing, who is pure, resourceful, unconcerned, unperturbed, and who indulges in no undertakings—that devotee of Mine is dear to Me.*)

A person who is neither interested in his own glorification nor is he perturbed due to any exigency, is skilful and harbours pure intentions is fit to be a true leader in the real sense of the word.

The word 'anapeksha', used in the previous shloka, indicates a person devoted to a higher cause, has absolutely no material desire for himself and is beyond any kind of craving or bias. He has no attachment to anything except doing his best to fulfil the divine design.

A true leader, according to the Gita, is one who is fully devoted to his dharma without having any ego or entertaining the sense of 'doership'. He looks at his role and his position, not as a symbol of power and authority, but as an opportunity to perform his prescribed duty and render service to the people. He does not consider himself to be a great leader and causes things to happen, acting simply as an instrument in the whole scheme of things.

Finally, Krishna, describes the ideal leader as one who transcends emotional extremes:

यो न हृष्यति न द्वेष्टि न शोचति न कांक्षति।
शुभाशुभपरित्यागी भक्तिमान्यः स मे प्रियः।।

(अध्याय 12/17)

Yo na hrishyati na dveshti na shochati na kaankshati.
Shubhaashubhaparityaagi bhaktimaanyah sa me priyah.

(Chapter 12/17)

(*He who neither rejoices nor despairs, who neither laments nor hankers, who has renounced good and evil deeds and is full of devotion, is dear to Me.*)

The previous shloka refers to a person who does not rejoice in mundane worldly pleasures and also does not grieve over sorrows. Such a person is neither perturbed due to any loss nor overjoyed with materialistic gains. He is beyond the feelings of both good and evil as he performs all actions as his offerings to God and does not have any selfish motive.

A leader having such virtues is able to render true service to the community and his organisation without any favour or malice, and is not deterred by adverse circumstances or unfavourable consequences. He performs all his duties with complete integrity and competence and has no attachment with the actions or the consequences thereof.

Key Learnings

- A true leader gives his best to the task at hand and works with complete love and devotion.
- According to the Gita, divine destiny ordains all, and we are but instruments in a much larger game plan.
- A leader who serves without any attachment and expectation is able to deeply connect with the people.
- The victory of the righteous who act according to dharma, and the annihilation of the unrighteous, is the essence of the divine design.
- The divine design aimed at establishing the supremacy of truth and justice ultimately wins the day, whatever the odds or the difficulties.
- A true leader performs his duties with complete integrity and competence having no attachment with the actions or the outcomes.
- The greatest leaders live not for power, but for purpose—and leave behind a lasting legacy.

•••••

Success Mantra **18**

Rising Above Passion

According to the Gita, a human being conducts his life's business under the influence of three intrinsic psycho-physical forces – tamas, rajas and sattva which govern the mind and shape outward actions. Tamas stands for the dominant inclination of an individual towards sloth, inertia and ignorance; rajas indicate the quality of passion and dynamism under influences of desire and attachment; and sattva denotes goodness and the illuminating aspects of a human being.

A person is known by his thoughts and actions, which, in essence depend on the consequent sum total of these forces impinging on his personality, and find expression in his beliefs and outward conduct. The secret to the success of a leader is how well he is able to synthesise these gunas in his being, regulate their interplay, and enhance/transcend their influences.

Krishna exhorts Arjuna to understand and harness these three modes of nature, tamas, rajas and sattva, which ultimately affect the thoughts and conduct of a person. A true leader should balance and regulate the interplay of these three modes to successfully perform his role in various exigencies that he encounters in life. Success lies in enhancing sattvik forces and mitigating tamasik intents.

Krishna tells Arjuna about the interplay of these modes of nature in the life of an individual:

सत्वं रजस्तम इति गुणाः प्रकृतिसम्भवाः
निबध्नन्ति महाबाहो देहे देहिनमव्ययम्।

(अध्याय 14/5)

Satvam rajastam iti gunaah prakritisambhavaa
Nibadhnanti mahaabaaho dehe dehinamvyayam.

(Chapter 14/5)

(*O mighty armed one! Sattva, rajas and tamas, these modes born of nature bind down the imperishable soul to the body.*)

These modes define the dominant trait of a human being. His thoughts, actions and responses depend on the predominance of a particular mode in his being. In brief, sattva is perfect purity and light, rajas is passion and activity-oriented, and tamas represents inertia and darkness. According to the Gita, when the inner being of a person identifies itself with any particular mode, it reflects the dominant tendency of that mode in his beliefs and deeds, and it creates some sort of bondage.

They trigger different thoughts and actions, and lead to different consequences. The interplay of these modes and the resulting responses depend upon one's intrinsic beliefs, external circumstances, memories of previous lives, and one's efforts to control base intents and elevate one's life.

A true leader has to practise the art of controlling these modes to ensure right thought, right speech and right action. Only then he can lead his organisation to success that is based on sound principles. A true leader, conscious of the adverse effects of excessive tamasik and rajasik intents, conducts himself in a balanced manner and retains control over the resulting responses of the interplay of modes, or else, the modes will go their own way and create their own trap and bondage.

The effects and consequences of these modes are very well explained in the following three shlokas:

तत्र सत्वं निर्मलत्वात्प्रकाशकमनामयम्।
सुखसंगेन बध्नाति ज्ञानसंगेन चानघ।।

(अध्याय 14/6)

Tatra sattvam nirmalatvaatprakaashakamanaamayam
Sukhasangen badhnaati jnaanasangen chanagha.

(Chapter 14/6)

(*O Arjuna, of these, sattva, the mode of goodness being purest, illuminating and flawless, binds the soul by attaching it to happiness and knowledge.*)

रजो रागात्मकं विद्धि तृष्णासंगसमुदभ्वम्।
तन्निबध्नाति कौन्तेय कर्मसंगेन देहिनम्।।

(अध्याय 14/7)

Rajo raagaatmakam viddhi trishnaasangasamudbhavam
Tannibadhnaati Kaunteya karmasangena dehinam.

(Chatper 14/7)

(O son of Kunti, know the rajas to be of the nature of passion born of craving and attachment. It binds the soul by attachment to action.)

तमस्त्वज्ञानजं विद्धि मोहनं सर्वदेहिनाम्।
प्रमादालस्यनिद्राभिस्तन्निबध्नाति भारत।।

(अध्याय 14/8)

Tamastvajnaanajam viddhi mohanam sarvadehinaam
Pramaadaalasyanidraabhistannibadhnaati Bhaarata.

(Chapter 14/8)

(O Bharata, know tamas to be born of ignorance as the cause of delusion for all embodied beings. It binds the soul through negligence, laziness and sleep.)

According to the Gita, sattva represents serenity, awakening and light. It is reflected by the virtuous personality with intellect and knowledge as the defining elements of one's being. This mode makes a person serene, tranquil, content, helpful and compassionate. It leads to good health, a peaceful demeanour and a kind persona. Although sattva creates joy and wellness, attachment to this mode also binds the soul to the material world.

The rajas guna also binds the soul to material existence as the obvious manifestations of this mode are spirited activities and passionate efforts. But its main inspiration is from cravings and attachments to the material world. This guna represents a wide spectrum of desires like lust, wealth, prestige, power, as well as the advancement of family, career and clan. It leads to a vicious cycle of passion and desire with no end to the cravings, and traps the soul in its web of worldly allure and physical possessions.

The mode of tamas is the antithesis of the sattva guna, and its dominant manifestations are pursuit of pleasure through laziness, intoxication, excessive sleep and having a total lack of balance and discretion. It is born of ignorance and darkness, as a person having dominant tamasik nature has no sense of right and wrong, moral and ethical behaviour, and the adverse consequences ensuing from such a conduct for himself, his family, community and the society he lives in. The people of tamsik nature ignore their duties and are found to be excessively attached to sloth and sleep. This mode in its extreme aspects represents all thoughts and deeds that negate the truth, the good and the beautiful, which should be the objective of human life. This mode creates its own delusion and leads to a pattern of gloom, grief, depression and suffering.

An alert and enlightened leader should be conscious about the effect of these three forces and ever cautious to avoid the trap of tamasik forces as well as the influence and allurement of rajasik inclinations. Keeping in mind the ruling consequences of individual modes, one can properly balance their interplay as has been preached and practised by various seers and sages through ages. Lord Buddha talks about adopting the *madhyam marg*, the middle path. The Gita also extols the qualities of being *sthitaprajna* and *gunaateet*, exercising balance and equanimity in one's thoughts and conduct. This can be developed with due contemplation, reading good scriptures, keeping the right company and the rigorous practice of penance and retrospection.

Krishna asks Arjuna to transcend the bondages of above mentioned three gunas:

गुणानेतानतीत्य त्रीन्देही देहसमुदभवान्
जन्ममृत्युजरादुःखैर्विमुक्तोऽमृतमश्नुते।

(अध्याय 14/20)

Gunaanetaanateetya treendehee dehsamudbhavaan
Janmamrityujaraaduhkhairvimukto mritamaashnute.

(Chapter 14/20)

(*By transcending these three modes, one gains freedom from birth, death, old age and sorrows, and attains immortality.*)

This shloka indicates that by avoiding the traps of these modes, one can obtain eternal wisdom. Being fully alert and aware, one can overcome rajasik and tamasik inclinations by enhancing and consolidating sattvik attributes in one's personality. This shloka talks about a stage when one can transcend even the attraction of sattvic gunas and realise the ultimate truth. This is the possibility of human evolution as described by Krishna in the Gita and should be the sole aim of human endeavour. This state gives absolute freedom from all bondage and suffering resulting from the cycle of life and death.

It is evident from the previous shlokas that transcending the traps of these modes one attains the real freedom. Almost all the religions and scriptures of the world have stated it to be the chief good and ultimate goal of human life. These shlokas have a profound message, not only for those desirous of spiritual attainment but also for all of us engaged in the daily survival of human existence. These are much more relevant for a leader who not only has to lead his own life with dignity and meaning, but also has the responsibility of guiding and leading the destiny of an organisation. The quality of rising above the traps of these modes and being and remaining the master of one's fate and captain of one's soul are, indeed, great attributes and tall objectives for a great leader.

The questions then arise, of how to achieve this state of being and what are the characteristics of a person who has transcended these modes of nature. In the following shloka, Arjuna asks Krishna to describe the attributes of such a person:

कैर्लिंगैस्त्रीन्गुणानेतानतीतो भवति प्रभो
किमाचारः कथं चैतांस्त्रीन्गुणानतिवर्तते।
(अध्याय 14/21)

Kairlingaistreengunaanetaanateeto bhavati prabho
Kimaachaarah katham chaitaanstreengunaanativartate.
(Chapter 14/21)

(*What are the characteristics of one who has risen above the three modes, and O Lord, how does he act and rise beyond the bondage of these gunas?*)

These are very simple but pertinent questions regarding the virtues, conduct and ways by which a person who has risen above these three modes of nature is distinguished.

Krishna tells Arjuna that a person who is not disturbed by the interplay of the gunas and remains steadfast in his belief, considers pain and pleasure alike and takes praise and censure to be the same, is said to have transcended all three modes of nature.

Krishna, to allay Arjuna's doubts further, explains the qualities of such a person:

मानापमानयोस्तुल्यस्तुल्यो मित्रारिपक्षयोः
सर्वारम्भपरित्यागी गुणातीतः स उच्यते।
(अध्याय 14/25)

Maanaapamaanayostulyastulyo mitraaripakshayoh
Sarvaarambhaparityaagi gunaateetah sa uchyate.
(Chapter 14/25)

(*He who is the same in honour and dishonour, the same to friends and foes, and has abandoned all enterprises is said to have risen above the modes.*)

According to the Gita, these attributes constitute the distinguishing marks of a *gunaateet* person, one who has risen above all the three modes of nature that bind a person with his body and intellect.

It is, indeed, a tall order for any human being encumbered by material existence, but it does indicate the direction in which a person or a leader desiring to use his full potential and serve the society should proceed. Even travelling some distance on the path of light and wisdom creates its own momentum and ultimately results in good deeds and the well-being of all. A leader who sincerely understands and endeavours to internalise these characteristics and acts accordingly is sure to serve his cause well and achieve distinction in thoughts, actions and repute.

The most important message of the above shlokas for a leader is to be alert and vigilant about the 'push and pull' of these three gunas; tamasik qualities have their pushes which degrade a person, the rajasik allure of wealth, power and passion as well as the traps of the sattvik gunas have very strong pull. The best course for a leader is to be above the charms of material objects as well as the hunger for name and fame. The core value for a leader is to be 'equipoised' and serve the people taking it as an opportunity, an act of sacrifice and a challenge to elevate and enlighten the self.

Key Learnings

- A person conducts himself according to the interplay of tamas, rajas, and sattva gunas.
- The sattva represents serenity, awakening and light reflected by a virtuous personality having intellect and knowledge as its defining elements.

- The rajas guna represents a wide spectrum of material desires like wealth, prestige and power having restless ambition as its defining element.
- The tamas mode reflects total lack of balance and discretion having dominant manifestations are of pursuit of pleasure through laziness, intoxication and excessive sleep.
- A leader is known by his vision and actions, which, in essence, depend on the consequent sum total of these forces impinging on his personality.
- According to the Gita, when the inner being of a person identifies itself with a particular mode, it reflects the dominant tendency of that mode in his beliefs and deeds.
- A true leader has to practise the art of balancing these modes to ensure right thoughts, right speech and right action.

•••••

Success Mantra **19**

Let Scriptures be Your Guide

The faith and belief of a person affect his thoughts, speech and actions. All of us work within our own sphere of influence. The collective traits of individuals in a society shape the culture, quality of life, direction and the future. A true leader must understand the situation, evaluate it and provide guidance to steer society towards desirable ends while curbing tendencies that are deleterious to social good.

Dr Martin Luther King Jr once said, "In a real sense, all life is inter-related. All men are caught in an inescapable network of mutuality, tied in a single garment of destiny. Whatever affects one directly, affects all indirectly. I can never be what I ought to be until you are what you ought to be, and you can never be what you ought to be until I am what I ought to be... This is the inter-related structure of reality."

It is true that to ensure a just, fair and prosperous society, all stakeholders have to work in tandem. It is an ideal situation and generally not achieved in reality. There arises the role of leaders.

Leaders are called upon to promote the common good, resolve conflicts, build new bridges, displace fear with courage, despair with hope, replace injustice with justice and make determined efforts to present a new road map for the better future of the organisation, society or the country, as the case may be. It is the main role of a visionary leader to see such new dreams and lead their organisation in its direction, as would have been impossible for any common man to do so.

Krishna emphasises the importance of an enlightened leadership, especially during times of adversity:

यदा यदा हि धर्मस्य ग्लानिर्भवति भारत।
अभ्युत्थानमधर्मस्य तदात्मानं सृजाम्यहम्।।

(अध्याय–4/7)

Yadaa yadaa hi dharmasya glaanirbhavati Bharata.
Abhyutthaanamadharmasya tadaatmaanam srijaamyaham.

(Chapter 4/7)

(*Whenever righteousness is on the decline and unrighteousness is in the ascendance, O Bharata, at that time I manifest Myself.*)

Dharma is nothing but a code of desirable conduct that is conducive to happiness and harmony in society and spiritual growth of individual human beings. In a way, it is the ordained duty of a person to act in full conformity with tradition and scriptures.

According to the Gita, whenever there is decline of righteousness and predominance of evil forces, God manifests Himself in human form. It is believed that whenever chaos and conflict prevail in society and evil forces are on the rise, divine forces intervene and some timeless leader emerges on the scene to re-establish order and justice. Krishna says that for the protection of the good and destruction of the wicked, and for the establishment of righteousness, He comes into being from age to age.

The Gita says that to resolve the situation arising from the conflict of divine and devilish forces, and to strengthen and establish justice and righteousness on a firm footing, divine forces work to correct the situation. A visionary and charismatic leader emerges in such circumstances, and by uprooting and destroying the evil forces, establishes the order of truth and justice in society.

There has been an ongoing conflict between divine and demonic forces since ages, and at critical juncture there comes an enlightened leader who by his thoughts and deeds strengthens the righteous and destroys the forces of evil.

Krishna elaborates on the contrasting characteristics of these two forces in the following shloka:

दैवी सम्पद्विमोक्षाय निबन्धायासुरी मता।
मा शुचः सम्पदं दैवीमभिजातोऽसि पाण्डव।।

(अध्याय 16/5)

Daivee sampadvimokshaaya nibandhaayaasuree mataa
Maa shuchah sampadam daiveemabhijaatosi Pandava.

(Chapter 16/5)

(*Divine qualities lead to liberation, while demonic qualities lead to bondage. Grieve not, O Pandava, for you are born with divine qualities.*)

The central theme of the Gita is to exhort Arjuna to eliminate the bondage of materialistic world and seek true freedom. This is said to be the chief objective of human life. The previous shloka further emphasises the role of such forces that lead to eternal freedom from bondage or trap a person in the ever-perpetuating cycle of life and death. The pursuit of divine virtues leads to truth and light whereas the demonic tendencies create the bondage of attachment and a keen desire for worldly objects.

The Gita describes various characteristics of divine and demonic forces, and specifies that vigour, forgiveness, fortitude, purity and freedom from malice are the attributes of a person born with divine qualities. On the other hand, hypocrisy, pride, anger, harshness, arrogance, violence and ignorance are the hallmarks of a person born with a demonic nature.

Krishna further describes the characteristics of a demonic disposition:

प्रवृत्तिं च निवृत्तिं च जना न विदुरासुराः
न शौचं नापि चाचारो न सत्यं तेषु विद्यते।

(अध्याय 16/7)

Pravrittin cha nivrittin cha janaa na viduraasuraah
Na shaucham naapi chaachaaro na satyam teshu vidyate.

(Chapter 16/7)

(*Men of demonic disposition cannot distinguish between right and wrong. Neither purity, nor right conduct, nor truth is found in them.*)

The Gita is a unique scripture that emphasises not only spiritual development and evolution of human beings, but is also greatly concerned with happiness and harmony in society. Dharma in the Gita is a set of duties or codes of conduct for a person to ensure the prevalence of truth and justice in society. It eulogises the divine virtues of people and denounces evil-doers throughout the discourse of the Gita.

People having demonic tendencies are completely ignorant about the right conduct and that which should be despised and loathed. History is full of such characters who by their thoughts and deeds caused great pain and suffering to mankind and ultimately met their doom. Their attributes have been listed in the previous shloka as being ignorant about the propriety of their actions and having neither purity, nor good conduct, nor truthfulness in their thoughts and actions.

Krishna, continuing his discourse in the Gita, further enlightens Arjuna about people with demonic leanings:

एतां दृष्टिमवष्टभ्य नष्टात्मानोऽल्पबुद्धयः
प्रभवन्त्युग्रकर्माणः क्षयाय जगतोऽहिताः।

(अध्याय 16/9)

Etaam drishtimavashtabhaya nashtaatmaanolpabuddhayah
Prabhavantyugrakarmaanah kshayaaya jagatohitaah.

(Chapter 16/9)

(*Holding this view, these slow-witted people of evil design perform destructive actions that harm the world.*)

According to the Gita the deeds of demonic people cause tremendous damage and suffering to others, and encourage and strengthen undesirable elements in society. People of demonic leanings do not believe in the eternal wisdom of truth and virtue and develop their own self-serving philosophy with the sole intent of possessing power and riches. They are given to impose their misguided and misleading views upon other people through various means and sources.

This has been clearly demonstrated throughout human history and has caused tremendous loss and damage to life, property, peace and harmony in the world. Twentieth century witnessed immense loss of life and property due to two World Wars, and decades-long Cold War, and innumerable regional conflicts. This was caused due to distorted notions and bloated egos of megalomaniac dictators, kings and leaders. They were motivated only by their perverse ambitions and blind desire for spreading their power and influence; they were least concerned with the consequent damage and devastation to the world. This hunger for power is evident even today, and, in fact, it has become worse.

It is often observed that leaders endowed with divine qualities are better positioned to influence large numbers of people—and for a longer duration—than those driven by demonic tendencies. Only such noble leaders can usher in a new era, transform society, and leave an enduring imprint on the sands of time.

Krishna cautions Arjuna about the three great vices that lead people astray – lust, anger and greed:

त्रिविधं नरकस्येदं द्वारं नाशनमात्मनः ।
कामः क्रोधस्तथा लोभस्तस्मादेतत्त्रयं त्यजेत् ।।

(अध्याय 16/21)

Trividham narakasyedam dvaaram naashanamaatmanah.
Kaamah krodhastathaa lobhastasmaadetattrayam tyajet.

(Chapter 16/21)

(*Lust, anger and greed—these are the three gates to hell which degrade the soul. These three, therefore, must be shunned.*)

Having explained the nature and conduct of people with demonic tendencies, Krishna forewarns Arjuna about the causes that are responsible for such leanings. He apprises Arjuna about three great vices namely lust, anger and greed that spoil and pollute the mind of a person, and refers to them as the three gates to hell, which invariably bring about the downfall of a person. Therefore, Krishna cautions Arjuna about them and tells him to shun these three evils. It is explained in the Gita that it is lust and greed which transform into anger and these three together are the greatest enemy of the people in the world.

There are numerous instances where immensely exalted sages and saints deviated from their chosen virtuous paths and fell from grace after falling under the influence of any one of these vices. These evils cause one to deviate from the path of truth and right conduct and therefore, it is necessary to give up these iniquities.

The Gita emphasises the importance of inculcating divine attributes and eliminating demonic propensities to fill the world with peace and harmony. It describes in great detail the habits of lust, greed and anger and the various thoughts and actions of people indulging in these vices, along with the ensuing consequences. Such people are ever obsessed with their ego, arrogance, lust and anger, and create misery and suffering for themselves as well as for others. Such conceited and haughty people, intoxicated by wealth and worldly acclaim, perform various sacrifices and acts of charity with the intention to just show off to the world.

They do not have any real respect for norms and virtues or concern and feelings towards anyone other than their own family and friends.

The following shloka highlights the consequences of not adhering to the precepts of the scriptures:

य: शास्त्रविधिमुत्सृज्य वर्तते कामकारत: ।
न स सिद्धिमवाप्नोति न सुखं न परां गतिम् ।।

(अध्याय 16 / 23)

Yah shaastravidhimutsrijya vartate kaamakaaratah.
Na sa siddhimavaapnoti na sukham na paraam gatim.

(Chapter 16/23)

(*He who forsakes the teachings of the scriptures and acts under the impulse of his selfish desire gains neither perfection, nor happiness, nor the highest state.*)

Therefore, a true leader must abide by the teachings of scriptures to ensure just and right conduct, irrespective of their context, time and space.

Krishna advises Arjuna to follow the wisdom of scriptures in all situations:

तस्माच्छास्त्रं प्रमाणं ते कार्याकार्यव्यवस्थितौ ।
ज्ञात्वा शास्त्रविधानोक्तं कर्म कर्तुमिहार्हसि ।।

(अध्याय 16 / 24)

Tasmaachchhaastram pramaanam te
kaaryaakaaryavyavasthitau.
Jnaatvaa shaastravidhaanok- tam karma kartumihaarhasi.

(Chapter 16/24)

(*Let the scripture be your guide in determining what should be done and what should not. Knowing the wisdom of the scriptures, you must act accordingly.*)

Krishna exhorts Arjuna to follow the path laid down by scriptures and act accordingly, as they provide the best guidelines for righteous actions and virtuous life. Whenever a dilemma arises, act according to the wisdom of the scriptures as only scriptures are the tried, tested and trusted repository of wisdom and right solutions.

Therefore, a leader should be well aware of the eternal wisdom enshrined in scriptures and act accordingly as they can provide guidance about the appropriate path to be followed in the twists and turns of life. A true leader should fully control the drive of ego and desire in the light of the intellect and wisdom contained in the scriptures and should never ever permit lust, anger and greed to influence his thoughts and actions. This is true for everybody, more so for a person in a position of leadership and authority, to avoid the pitfalls and the ever-deepening trap of lust, anger and greed. Only then can one follow the path of virtue and divinity and abstain from demonic traits and leanings.

Key Learnings

- The prevailing traits of people in a society shape the culture, quality of life, direction, and ultimately, the future of that society.
- A true leader must understand situations, evaluate them, and guide towards desirable ends while curbing harmful tendencies.
- A true leader must promote the common good, resolve conflicts, build hope, and work towards justice, and a better future.
- Dharma in the Gita is nothing but a code of desirable conduct that is conducive to peace and harmony in society and for the spiritual growth of the individual.
- A leader with divine qualities is in a better position to affect the activities of a large number of people for a longer time, as compared to one who has demonic leanings.

- A true leader must control their ego and desire and never permit lust, anger and greed to influence his thoughts and actions.

•••••

Success Mantra 20

Action Without Faith is Futile

Faith is the intrinsic make-up—the internal structure of values, beliefs, preferences, prejudices and intuition—that affects the thoughts and actions of an individual. Faith enables us to believe what the reasoning faculties refuse to.

Kahlil Gibran says, "Faith is knowledge within the heart, beyond the reach of proof." while William Wordsworth describes it as, "a passionate intuition."

Martin Luther King Jr. observes, "Faith is taking the first step even when you don't see the whole staircase." Faith provides an inner reservoir of courage, hope, confidence, calmness and trust that propels a leader to proceed even amidst the most adverse situations.

It is said that the faith of a person does not necessarily depend upon his personal experience, acquired knowledge and scriptural wisdom, but is a function of his belief and character. The thoughts and actions of a person depend upon his faith, which rules all his beliefs, behaviour and responses.

In the Gita, there occurs a very interesting dialogue between Arjuna and Krishna, where Arjuna asks about the position of those who do not act according to the wisdom of the scriptures but are endowed with strong faith.

Krishna tells Arjuna that faith is a function of the essence, the inner being and the intrinsic nature of a person:

सत्त्वानुरूपा सर्वस्य श्रद्धा भवति भारत ।
श्रद्धामयोऽयं पुरुषो यो यच्छ्रद्धः स एव सः ।।

(अध्याय 17/3)

Sattvaanurupaa sarvasya shraddhaa bhavati Bharata.
Shraddhaamayo'yam purusho yo yachchhraddhah sa eva sah.

(Chapter 17/3)

(*O Arjuna! The faith of every individual is in accord with his innate character. Man is made of faith; as is his faith, so is he.*)

The destiny and the direction of a person's life depend on his faith. The intensity of his faith and his inner commitments decide the path he will take—whether he will travel along the beaten track or take the one less traveled, or the one never travelled before.

Krishna describes three kinds of faith: sattvik, rajasik and tamasik. Accordingly, there are three distinct kinds of people having sattvik, rajasik and tamasik leanings, and their actions largely conform to these tendencies. He further explains that the actions and conduct of a person are governed by his food, speech and disposition, and these in turn, mainly depend on his faith.

A person views the world and the people around according to his own faith, and his ways of worship, food, speech, thoughts and actions depend upon his faith. The Gita says that every man is born with a particular nature which shapes his faith. However, the leanings and choices that we nourish also affect our thoughts and actions. Therefore, it is always advisable to indulge in noble thoughts and lofty objectives.

The Gita categorises human actions, desires, tastes, charity, austerity, indeed everything into three groups, namely, sattvik, rajasik and tamasik. In sattvik people, the spirit of truth and harmony dominate, while in the rajasik, it is the passion and urge to act, and in the tamasik, inertia and ignorance dictate their thoughts and actions.

Krishna explains that these tendencies influence not just one's actions, but also one's food, sacrifice, penance and charitable acts:

आहारस्त्वपि सर्वस्य त्रिविधो भवति प्रियः
यज्ञस्तपस्तथा दानं तेषां भेदमिमं श्रृणु।

(अध्याय 17/7)

Aahaarastvapi sarvasya trividho bhavati priyah
Yajnastapastathaa daanam teshaam bhedamimam srinu.

(Chapter 17/7)

(*Even the likings for food are of three kinds. So are the sacrifices, austerities and charities. Hear, how they differ.*)

The Gita describes three kinds of penance—the penance of the body, speech and mind. Penance of the body is to worship gods, gurus and elders, and the observance of purity, abstinence and non-violence. Similarly, the penance of speech is using sweet and inoffensive, truthful and propitious words that cause annoyance to none, as well as the study and recitation of the scriptures.

Krishna, further advancing the description of penance of the body and speech, describes the penance of the mind:

मनःप्रसादः सौम्यत्वं मौनमात्मविनिग्रहः
भावसंशुद्धिरित्येतत्तपो मानसमुच्यते।

(अध्याय 17/16)

Manahprasaadah saumyatvam maunamaatmavinigrahah
Bhaavasamshuddhirityetattapo maanasamuchyate.

(Chapter 17/16)

(*Serenity of mind, gentleness, silence, self-restraint, and purity of feelings—these constitute penance of the mind.*)

Penance of the mind should be considered to be at a higher pedestal than that of the body and speech, because if the mind is mastered, the body and speech by themselves conform to the mind. It is the mind and the ensuing thoughts that determine an individual's consciousness, his beliefs and the direction of his life. The Gita emphasises that one should elevate oneself with the power of one's mind and never degrade oneself, for it is the mind that can be one's greatest friend or most fierce foe.

Penance of the mind constitutes the serenity of thoughts, balanced conduct, purity of purpose and a calm and quiet disposition. Being unperturbed even amidst the turmoil of the world represents an evolved state of mind. Serenity of thoughts is of utmost importance as they can make or mar a person, his destiny and life. Each thought that emerges on the mindscape, if pursued, determines our destiny. Therefore, there is tremendous emphasis in the Gita to keep a watch on the mind and develop a balanced and equanimous attitude towards life and the world.

These qualities endow a leader with deep insight and lofty vision and enable him to see new heights, new horizons and create a new world despite prevailing chaos and turmoil. Mahatma Gandhi, Abraham Lincoln and Nelson Mandela were leaders who actively exercised the penance of the mind and succeeded in creating a new world for their people. They also left behind a philosophy, vision and roadmap for posterity to follow and benefit from their thoughts and actions.

A great leader performs his actions with faith, commitment and conviction. Commitment and conviction result from deep faith in one's beliefs, thoughts and actions, as well as the objectives one is striving to achieve. Such a leader is true to himself and has complete faith in his thoughts, words and deeds. This requires an evolved mind, determined effort, and, above all, an abiding faith in the purity and goodness of the ends and the means being pursued.

Krishna, concluding about the importance of faith in human life, says the following:

अश्रद्धया हुतं दत्तं तपस्तप्तं कृतं च यत्।
असदित्युच्यते पार्थ न च तत्प्रेत्य नो इह।।

(अध्याय 17/28)

Ashraddhayaa hutamdattam tapastaptam kritam cha yat.
Asadityuchyate Partha na cha tatpretya no iha.

(Chapter 17/28)

(O Partha, an oblation offered, a gift given, a penance performed, or any other act done without faith is termed as naught, and is of no avail here or hereafter.)

Krishna exalts faith as fundamental to all our thoughts and actions, and declares that anything done without faith is valueless and has no meaning in this world or even beyond.

It is faith that determines the possibility of the highest evolution of a human being, be he an ordinary person or a leader; faith is the only element which leads one to organise his inner being and achieve even the highest, most divine and the noblest of the objectives he sets his eyes on. Faith enables a leader to act in accordance with his dharma, and devote his life to the service of community, society and the world to the best of his capability, and play a significant role in making the life of others better, enriched and sublime.

Key Learnings

- Faith is the intrinsic make-up—the internal structure of values, beliefs, preferences, prejudices and intuition that affects the thoughts and actions of an individual.
- Faith of a person does not necessarily depend upon his personal experience, acquired knowledge and scriptural wisdom, but is a function of his belief and character.
- A man is made up of his faith and cognitive perceptions, and it is one's faith that governs their leanings, thoughts and activities.
- A person views the world according to his own faith which determines their conduct, food, speech, thoughts and actions.
- According to Gita penance is threefold:

Of the body – through worship and purity

Of speech – through truth, gentleness, and study and recitation of scriptures.

Of the mind – through serenity, silence, self-discipline, and inner purity.

- Mastery of the mind leads to mastery of life. The mind, when calm and aligned with divine becomes the greatest friend of the self.
- The penances of the body, speech and mind endow a leader with deep insight and lofty vision, and enable them to transform themselves and the world.

•••••

Success Mantra **21**

Delusion Destroyed; Wisdom Gained

It is said that there is nothing more difficult, more perilous or more uncertain than to introduce a new concept, a new order and a new culture in an organisation.

It is a known fact that to achieve success on a sustainable basis, an organisation has to change with time. A great leader is one who is able to gauge the trends of the time and transform his organisation to face the emerging challenges. Each organisation reflects a unique ecosystem and realities of the people working together, and to affect major changes in the direction of its working and culture is always an uphill task. This is precisely the role of a truly great leader, who, if successful, acts as an example for others and is remembered for a long time.

It is a well-observed phenomenon that people resist change, more so when they have to change themselves, too. The poet W.H. Auden has aptly captured this dilemma:

We would rather be ruined than changed,
We would rather die in our dread
Than climb the cross of the moment
And let our illusions die.

In the Bhagavad Gita, Krishna's mission is to dissolve Arjuna's delusions and awaken him to the eternal truths of life. His effort has been to change the thought process and perceptions of Arjuna, the great warrior, and make him understands his duties in the circumstances. Krishna, through the wisdom of the Gita, tries to transform Arjuna and enable him to take an appropriate decision and act according to his dharma.

Krishna tells Arjuna that it is not advisable to abandon one's duty, either due to attachment or the fear of consequences:

नियतस्य तु संन्यासः कर्मणो नोपपद्यते
मोहात्तस्य परित्यागस्तामसः परिकीर्तितः।

(अध्याय 18/7)

Niyatasya tu sannyaasah karmano nopapadyate
Mohaattasya parityaagastaamasah parikeertitah.

(Chapter 18/7)

(It is not right to renounce one's prescribed duty. Its abandonment due to delusion is said to be an act of tamasik nature.)

According to the Gita, abandonment of any duty that ought to be done is not right. To abandon one's prescribed duty is understood to be an act of dullness and ignorance. The Gita does not approve the act of a person who gives up his duties for fear of physical strain and considers all actions painful. It lays great emphasis on the need to perform one's prescribed duties without any attachment to the actions or their fruits.

A leader has to motivate the people in his organisation to work towards set goals and not be distracted by minor incidents or lapses. He must also encourage them to keep themselves above their own self-interests. It is said that good leadership is the art of enabling even an average person to accomplish great tasks.

True leadership is motivating people even of average capabilities to realise their potential and do the work, which in their minds is well beyond their capabilities. It is said that greatness does not lie in achieving great things, but in doing even ordinary things with great love and extraordinary devotion. This is possible only when a leader himself attends to his given duties without any fear or favour, and leads his group to act accordingly.

The Gita describes the qualities of enlightened leadership in the following shloka:

मुक्तसंगोऽनहंवादी धृत्युत्साहसमन्वितः
सिद्धयसिद्धयोर्निर्विकारः कर्ता सात्विक उच्यते।

(अध्याय 18/26)

Muktasangonahamvaadee dhrityutsaahsamanvitah
Siddhyasiddhyornirvikaarah kartaa saatvik uchyate.

(Chapter 18/26)

(*One who is free from attachment, has no speech of egotism, endowed with firmness and zeal, and unaffected by success and failure is said to be a sattvik doer.*)

The Gita describes three categories of doers based on their virtues, conduct and mode of working. The doer who performs his duties with enthusiasm and determination does not cling to the actions or their fruits and is devoid of ego has been called a sattvik doer. These characteristics are of paramount importance for a leader who is determined to change the status quo and transform people in the organisation. To be a transformational leader, one has to understand himself, be true to his role and responsibilities, transcend his own interests, and keep the cause of his organisation uppermost in his mind.

The main task before such a leader is to motivate people through their thoughts, speech and actions to do their best and work for the highest good of all. Under the guidance and supervision of such an enlightened leader, people in the team feel highly elevated and empowered, and share aims and aspirations of the leader, willingly doing their best to achieve the objectives of the organisation.

An organisation that has transformational leadership at its apex does not get bogged down by obstacles and set- backs in its journey towards its destination. A true leader knows very well that the actions that seem painful and difficult in the beginning have immense potential for growth and evolution, and invariably lead to great success and achievements.

Krishna explains this paradoxical truth in the following shloka:

यत्तदग्रे विषमिव परिणामेऽमृतोपमम्।
तत्सुखं सात्त्विकं प्रोक्तमात्मबुद्धिप्रसादजम्।।

(अध्याय 18/37)

Yattadagre vishamiva parinaamemritopamam.
Tatsukham sattvikam proktamatmabuddhiprasadajam.

(Chapter 18/37)

(That which feels like poison in the beginning but turns to nectar in the end – that happiness, born of inner wisdom and true understanding of self is said to be sattvik.)

Happiness has been the universal aim of life for people since time immemorial. Happiness for different people means different things. The objects of happiness vary according to the mode which dominates the basic nature of a human being. If a person is of a tamasik nature, he derives happiness with inertia, intoxication and violent acts. If rajasik tendencies dominate the nature of a person, he will seek happiness in power, wealth, pride and fame. But according to the Gita, true happiness does not lie in possession of power, prestige and riches, but in the fulfilment of intellectual pursuits and elevation of a person's own self. This is called sattvik happiness.

The previous shloka describes that sattvik happiness results from acts that may appear hard and difficult in the beginning but the ensuing consequences are sweet and sublime, and provide the highest type of joy and happiness.

A true leader understands that acts that appear difficult and require crucial decision-making in the beginning generally lead to great success and unprecedented results. Such acts enable a person to realise his own strength and transform him for good, leading to great success and genuine happiness. All great leaders in history have been aware of this truth and have never hesitated in taking hard and painful decisions when the ultimate objectives were lofty and beneficial to the society.

The history of the world is witness to the fact that great campaigns, struggles for freedom, social reforms and the fight for the rights of the oppressed and downtrodden could be successful only because the leaders did not hesitate in taking hard and crucial decisions, and faced unparalleled pain and suffering in bringing out transformational changes and revolutionary outcomes.

It has been observed that revolutionary changes in human affairs in all parts of the world required transformational leadership and hard and long-drawn-out struggles. Challenging circumstances require a transformational leader who can take appropriate decisions even amidst most adverse circumstances, and lead his team with determined zeal and resolve. A transformational leader not only awakens the people and motivates them, but also leads from the front to walk his talk and affect the desired changes. It is the role of a transformational leader to make people stand on their feet, sustain the struggle in a united and organised manner and fight for their rights till the end.

After Arjuna refused to join the war and put down his bow and arrows, the greatest challenge before Krishna was how to correct his perceptions towards his duty and the call of the hour, and transform his beliefs and understanding about the realities of the situation. Krishna, during his long discourse, made gradual but sustained efforts to make Arjuna understand this. His sole effort was to expose and enlighten him to various alternate philosophies, wisdom of the scriptures, and understanding one's own self in the broader context of the universe. He exhorted Arjuna to evolve and develop a balanced and equanimous attitude towards life, and make the right decision in view of the wisdom and precepts of the scriptures. The main purpose of Krishna as a transformational leader in the given context was to guide Arjuna to reach some well thought-out and considered conclusions, and decide his next course of action.

Krishna, at the end of the discourse in the Gita, wanted to leave the final decision to Arjuna's own discretion.

All along, his aim was to awaken Arjuna, to make him understand his own self, to draw his attention to the precepts of the scriptures, and persuade him to follow his dharma. But in the divine scheme of things, nobody is compelled or driven to a conclusion as it has to be a person's free will, an act of his own choice.

Krishna at Kurukshetra was present in the role of a charioteer only and it was incumbent upon him to obey the direction that Arjuna chose. He tried to influence the conduct of Arjuna because of his love for him and the path of truth and righteousness being followed by the Pandavas. But Arjuna had to think for himself and take a call about his role in the given context of the war of the Mahabharata. He was expected to act on his own volition and conscience and take rational and appropriate decisions about his role.

Krishna at the culmination of his long discourse asks Arjuna to exercise his own choice about the next step:

इति ते ज्ञानमाख्यातं गुह्याद्गुह्यतरं मया।
विमृश्यैतदशेषेण यथेच्छसि तथा कुरु।।

(अध्याय 18/63)

Iti te gyanam akhyatam. guhyad guhyataram. maya.
vimr. ishyaitad ashes. hen. a yathechchhasi tatha kuru.

(Chapter 18/63)

(Thus, I have expounded the most mysterious of all secret knowledge. Reflect deeply on this, and act as you wish.)

Krishna calls the wisdom enshrined in the Gita as the most secret of the secret knowledge. In common parlance, a secret is the knowledge which is neither accessible nor known to majority of the people. The Gita describes in detail about the knowledge of the soul, knowledge of His own omniscient and omnipresent form and prowess, concept of yoga, laws of karma and importance of equanimity in life, etc. Above all, there is great emphasis on devotion and the concept of dharma in the Gita. In addition, Krishna has described the concepts of purush and prakriti and modes of nature that affect almost all aspects of human life. That is why he calls it the 'most secret of all secret knowledge', and asks him to reflect on it fully and act as per his own choice.

This is a very relevant lesson in the context of leadership, as a leader is always exposed to myriad sources of information, advice and knowledge. But a true leader should take a call based on his own discretion and should never blindly follow any advice or recommendation while attending to his duties as a leader of an organisation.

Krishna, at the end of the Gita, asks Arjuna if he has listened to the discourses of the Gita carefully and whether his delusion has been dispelled:

कच्चिदेतच्छ्रुतं पार्थ त्वयैकाग्रेण चेतसा।
कच्चिदज्ञानसम्मोहः प्रनष्टस्ते धनंजय।।

(अध्याय 18/72)

Kachchidetachchhrutam Partha tvayaikaagrena chetasaa.
Kachchhidajnaanasammohah pranashtaste Dhananjaya.

(Chapter 18/72)

(*O Partha, have you listened with focused mind? Has your delusion caused by ignorance been destroyed, O Dhananjaya?*)

Krishna was not only an embodiment of God, but he was also a transformational and enlightened leader in the true sense of the terms. He made the sincerest effort to dispel the delusion born of attachment and ignorance by replying to Arjuna's innumerable doubts and queries, and enlightening him about dharma, truth and reality. Krishna did not force any decision upon Arjuna, and as a great Guru, only tried to guide him in understanding his role in the light of his dharma. He endeavoured to expound the reality of truth and dharma to enable Arjuna in taking his own decision regarding further course of action. In the end, Krishna clearly asks Arjuna whether he has heard the Gita's discourses with attention and if his delusion born of ignorance has been dispelled.

Arjuna, the warrior of warriors, in response to the direct question asked by Krishna, his great friend, philosopher and mentor, replied in the affirmative:

नष्टो मोहः स्मृतिर्लब्धा त्वत्प्रसादान्मयाच्युत।
स्थितोऽस्मि गतसन्देहः करिष्ये वचनं तव।।

(अध्याय 18/73)

Nashto mohah smritirlabdha tvatprasaadaanmayaachyuta.
Sthitosmi gatasandehah karishye vachanam tava.

(Chapter 18/73)

(*O Achyuta, due to your grace, my delusion has been destroyed and I have regained my memory. I stand firm with my doubts dispelled, and shall act according to your command.*)

At the end of the discourse on the battlefield of Kurukshetra, Arjuna, in his concluding response, says that by the grace of Krishna, his delusion has been destroyed and wisdom has been restored. He further says that he is now willing to act as per the directions of Krishna. The clear declaration of Arjuna that his delusion caused by attachment and ignorance has been destroyed by the teachings of the Gita is a great lesson for mankind.

Krishna, concluding the discourse, further says that studying, contemplating and acting according to the wisdom of the Gita can destroy all doubts and lead a human being towards light and eternal wisdom.

At the end, there is a very interesting conclusion given by Sanjay, the narrator of the unfolding events at Kurukshetra and the ongoing dialogue between Krishna and Arjuna to King Dhritrashtra. In the concluding shloka of the Gita, Sanjay articulates a prophetic vision, presenting his assessment of the war's eventual outcome to King Dhritarashtra, even before the battle has commenced:

यत्र योगेश्वरः कृष्णो यत्र पार्थो धनुर्धरः।
तत्र श्रीर्विजयो भूतिर्ध्रुवा नीतिर्मतिर्मम।।

(अध्याय 18/78)

Yatra yogeshvarah Krishno yatra Partho dhanurdharah.
Tatra shrirvijayo bhutirdhruvaa nitirmatirmama.

(Chapter 18/78)

(*Wherever there is Krishna, the Lord of Yoga, and Arjuna, the wielder of the bow, there will surely be glory, victory, prosperity and unfailing righteousness— this is my conviction.*)

Sanjay declares that wherever Krishna and Arjuna are, glory, victory, righteousness, prosperity and good fortune shall reign supreme.

This point has been very well substantiated by numerous examples in history, where people leading their lives as per the precepts of the Gita realised their true potential and served humanity by creating a new life and a new world for millions of people across the world.

Mahatma Gandhi was first introduced to the Gita when he came across its famous English translation, Divine Song, by the eminent poet Sir Edwin Arnold. English poet Thomas Carlyle was most impressed with the Gita. The renowned American saint and author Henry David Thoreau is said to have worshipped the Gita. His ardent disciple, the American author Ralph Waldo Emerson, was a great admirer of this text as well.

The famous English poet T.S. Eliot has called the Gita 'the greatest treasure of mankind'.

Aldous Huxley commented on the Gita through the following words:

> "The Gita is one of the clearest and most comprehensive summaries of the perennial philosophy ever to have been made. Hence, its enduring value is of great significance not only for Indians, but for all mankind. The Bhagwad-Gita is perhaps the most systematic spiritual statement of the perennial philosophy."

Bal Gangadhar Tilak, Lala Lajpat Rai, Ram Prasad Bismil, Chandra Shekhar Azad, Bhagat Singh, Subhash Chandra Bose and many other revolutionaries of the Indian freedom struggle derived their inspirations from the Gita. Mahatma Gandhi, the great apostle of non-violence, also took refuge in it whenever his mind was agitated. All these examples speak volumes about the inclusiveness and greatness of the Gita, the scripture of scriptures.

Mahatma Gandhi wrote in *Young India*:

> "When disappointment stares me in the face, and all alone, I see not a ray of light, I go back to the Bhagavad-Gita. I find a verse here and a verse there, and I immediately begin to smile in the midst of overwhelming tragedies. My life has been full of external tragedies, and if they have left no visible or indelible scar on me, I owe it all to the teaching of Bhagavad-Gita. Those who meditate on the Gita will derive fresh joy and new meanings from it every day."

It is a well-observed fact that for everybody, whether a person leading a family, an organisation or a country—whatever be the role and status, the eternal wisdom of the Gita has unique significance in his life as friend, philosopher and divine voice that has stood the test of time for people in all parts of the world.

Thus, to lead a life of joy, meaning and substance, despite its constant twists and turns, there is no other scripture or guide book that compares to the Bhagavad Gita in context, content, analysis, logical flow, philosophy and conclusions regarding truth and divinity. Its wisdom has been duly witnessed and corroborated by seers and sages, as well as the commoners, through the ages.

Key Learnings

- There is nothing more difficult, more perilous, or more uncertain than to introduce a new concept, a new order and a new culture in an organisation.
- Each organisation reflects a unique ecosystem and distinct realities, and to introduce major changes in its culture and working is a great challenge.
- True leadership lies not in commanding the capable, but in awakening the potential of ordinary individuals – enabling them to achieve what they once believed was beyond them.
- It is wisely said, greatness does not lie in doing great things, but in doing small things with great love, sincerity, and devotion.
- A visionary leader understands that what appears painful in the beginning often carries the promise of growth and transformation.
- A transformational leader does not merely preach change – he embodies it, leads from the front, and inspires through personal example.

- Krishna did not dictate; he guided. He enabled Arjuna to rediscover his inner strength and act according to his dharma, fulfilling his role with conviction and understanding.
- The Bhagavad Gita remains unparalleled in its spiritual depth, philosophical clarity, and practical guidance. It continues to serve as a timeless manual for truth, duty, and enlightened leadership.

•••••

About the Author

An engineering graduate from IIT Roorkee and a distinguished officer of the Indian Administrative Service, J.S. Mishra is widely recognized as a competent administrator, an empowering leader, a thoughtful writer, and a passionate poet. To date, he has published 16 books, including seven collections of Hindi poetry, an anthology of English poems, two well-received books on happiness titled *Happiness is a Choice: Choose to be Happy*, and *The Art of Joyful Living*, and five other acclaimed works.

His poetry has resonated deeply with both literary connoisseurs and general readers, earning widespread appreciation. His earlier book on the Gita, *Art of Life: Timeless Wisdom from the Gita*, has been warmly received by readers across all age groups and has garnered praise from both lay readers and scholars of the Gita and Vedic philosophy.

J.S. Mishra's contributions have been recognized through numerous literary awards, state honours, and citations for his outstanding achievements in both professional and literary spheres.

He is currently serving as Chancellor, Sushant University, Gurugram, Haryana.